My Father, Sandy

Nicholas Wollaston

✳ SHORT BOOKS

First published in 2003 by
Short Books
15 Highbury Terrace
London N5 1UP

10 9 8 7 6 5 4 3 2 1

A CIP catalogue record for this book
is available from the British Library.

ISBN 1-904095-44-5

Printed by Biddles Ltd.,
Guildford, Surrey

'no man climbs so high as he who does
not know where he is going'

Oliver Cromwell

*M*y father's name was Alexander Frederick Richmond Wollaston. For a study of his life, more a memoir than a biography, though I have few memories of him, I find it hard to decide what to call him. 'My father' begins to cloy when repeated often on the page, and simply 'Father', which is how my mother spoke of him to me and my sisters, seems pious. Plain 'Wollaston' is what his contemporaries – late Victorians, Edwardians, male and female – called him, but it now sounds cold and bald. Feeling both near him and sadly distant I have settled for 'Sandy', the name his family and close friends used, though I could never have called him that myself.

Likewise my mother, Mary Amelia Meinertzhagen – whose marriage to him was deeply loving though miserably brief – must be simply 'Mary'.

Alexander Frederick Richmond Wollaston, Dutch New Guinea, 1912

I TO THE BEYOND

At teatime in the dining-room he lifted me on to his knee and helped himself to more quince jam. 'Well Bill, my boy...' he said. My middle name is William but nobody else has used it. It was a privilege, almost a pledge, to live up to. I was his son, the inheritor of something I would never grow to understand.

A week before, in the summer of 1930, we had moved to Cambridge. To this house near his college. There was a sense of beginning, and no intimation whatever of an end. No clouds to darken the picture. He was fifty-five, old for the father of two small daughters and a son, but far too young to die. I was nearly four, my elder sister was five, my younger sister only two. Behind him in the corner of the room was the cabinet with his collection of butterflies, moths, bird's eggs from around the world. On the mantelpiece a family clock ticked and chimed insistently. A tolling bell? More likely a reminder of the children's bedtime. Through the French windows the garden, which we had explored with approval, awaited his passion for planting, his eye for the true, his dislike of the pretentious. The fussy rose beds in the lawn had been grassed over, the veranda demolished to bring light into the house. At the head of the table with the tea things Mary – his wife, our mother – poured him another cup while he spooned quince jam from a blue china pot to his plate. It was his favourite jam.

So who was he, this man in tweeds whose knee I sat on? He had a silk handkerchief in his pocket, a signet ring on his finger. Was there a suspicion of lavender water? Or a father's smile? A chuckle? I am not sure. I can see him in photos – posed stiffly for a studio portrait or wearing shorts and puttees in a jungle or bearded in a mountain camp. But I can't catch his voice or his laugh, or get round the back to look at the other side. And the flood of eulogy that was soon to come rolling in stays obstinately unrevealing.

He was of the very best stuff that explorers are made of, in the view of a famous veteran who knew what he was talking about. To others he was the staunchest of companions, a lover of every living thing, a master of himself to a rare degree, the embodiment of all the beauty and wisdom that a happy warrior conveys. They spoke of his private reticence but gift for friendship, his noble character and manly courage, his equal command of men of action or of intellect, civilized or primitive. His eye and his voice, someone said, lent enhancement to things both great and small, but they are lost on me. To a Cambridge don his disarming humour, such a pleasure in the quiet of a college, would be meat and drink to anyone with him in the stress of outlandish places. Another looked back on a friendship with him as one of the few great things of life. I am no wiser. I only wish I could have joined his multitude of friends.

Though they rejoiced in his successes they regretted the frequent disappearances, the long absences. They were proud of him and never doubted his power of pulling through. But when he came home they felt he belonged to another dimension from which they were excluded. And trying to fix him in words for an obituary one of them pointed to a rare excellence that was hard to put down. Ah, I feel – that's more like it. Something that escaped the first impressions, the glib applause. Something wild but intensely human that, as a novelist, I should recognize.

A sharp old lady of ninety-four could still see him coming to her room when she was a girl of fourteen in bed with flu, enchanting her with tales of the mountain wilderness he had just come back from and a flowering tree he had seen there. He was delightful, she told me, recalling her love for him long ago. But he could be severe, quarrelsome – or too aloof to bother – and liked people who stood up to him. He craved hard facts and honest truths, she said, and seemed to draw comfort from deprivation, fatigue, rigour. So I begin to perceive a side which others missed or ignored.

They praised his uncommon life, but none of them had foretold his unimaginable death. Though I sometimes wonder, was there no hint of the tragedy to come? No ominous rumbles to threaten his story's prologue? No warning shadow to creep across the page? He himself that summer afternoon in Cambridge, reunited with his family at last, could have had no fear of any sudden trick of fate. After surviving danger in far corners of the earth, to be marked now as the target for murder was absurd to the point of denial. In this gentle scene of harmony Mary alone – just possibly, I think – was uneasy, sensing the imminent ghost of destiny, a whisper in the air.

When did I last see my father?

Sandy, shortly before he died, with his three children, Joanna, Georgina and Nicholas

At teatime, is the real answer – watching him eat bread and butter with quince jam. But reality is not all. I am twenty years older than he was that day. Would he and I have quarrelled as I grew up? Can I find words to trap the man behind the fame? I can only offer a sort of love letter, a declaration of feelings difficult to articulate. From his knee I looked up at a father who would be elusive, impalpable, a lasting myth. It became my final vision of him. A blurred, oblique vignette from the last days of his life, preserved for the rest of mine.

***

Sandy was born in 1875 at Clifton near Bristol, one of eight children. His father was a housemaster at Clifton College, an inspiring but stern teacher of the things a cultivated boy should know. His mother was a Richmond, a family of painters descended from the landlord of a pub at Kew. Their home was described as 'overflowing with music and conversation and hospitality', which suggests a hothouse of highbrow austerity, stinging wit, intolerance for anyone too dim to keep up. Sandy's only brother escaped to a fruit farm in Canada and died an old bachelor in the Vancouver Club. Of six sisters – clever, proud, intimidating women – three found husbands but had no children, the others stayed spinsters: my vigilant, stiff-necked aunts. The mood in that schoolmaster's household may have helped drive Sandy on his travels.

Sandy as a young boy

After prep school and five years at Clifton College – where a beating was doubly humiliating from his father-housemaster – it was a wonderful release to reach Cambridge. There, at King's College, Sandy found a new home, a new world. A fresh, expansive society in the college and freedom to roam the countryside. As a boy he had filled a diary with notes on birds observed – the first nightingale of spring, a whinchat's nest with six eggs, the variations in song between a marsh and reed and sedge warbler – and now he could follow the call of a born naturalist. Though he missed the balmy West Country air and didn't care for the fogs and chills of East Anglia – 'the most deadly climate I was ever in' – he fell for the beauty of Cambridge, its great trees and sunsets. And in spite of shyness – 'it takes some time for me to know people' – he made friends who would last his life.

He studied Natural Sciences with extra geology and biology, and complained of 'a frightful amount of work'. But for academic success he spent too much time watching swallows building nests by the town bathing-sheds, or marvelling at a sandpiper flying under the college bridges, or basking at Byron's Pool, listening for a corn bunting. He bicycled into the fens to study the curious drumming made by a snipe's tail feathers, and to Suffolk for a stone curlew's nest and Norfolk for terns and water rails. He found joy in plants too – aconites along the Backs, a field of cowslips at the end of a cycle ride, the budding quince at King's. And he collected butterflies and moths as well as eggs.

After three years of desultory but happy study Sandy graduated in 1896 with a pass degree, the lowest class. It hardly mattered; he had no wish to be a don but stayed at King's two more years. Later he wrote to a younger sister in the throes of her Cambridge finals: 'I remember waking up to the fact that it was too late to begin work, so I settled into a sort of philosophic calm and enjoyed the term as much as any other, except during the days of the exam when the weather was very hot and I would fain have been elsewhere. Fortunately the friends you make at Cambridge are worth all the firsts and all the triposes that ever tripped – or I was particularly blessed.'

From the beginning King's College held a peculiar importance for him. Long after leaving it, lying with fever in Africa, he noted, 'December 6th, St Nicholas and our pious founder

Henry VI. Thought much of King's and the peaceful beauty there. Drank *In piam memoriam* in a glass of Congo port.' Later still, cutting through the New Guinea jungle, he wrote to a friend in the college, 'December 6th – give my love to King's. It's an odd thing, but King's is where I feel more firmly rooted than anywhere else.' Wherever he was, he seldom failed to toast the feast-day of the college's patron saint after whom, near the end of his life, he named his only son – me.

As a child aware of people's expectations, I was given an egg-blowing outfit, a butterfly net and killing bottle, a note-book for entering the birds I saw. But the father I had never had was the man I would never be. When a woodpecker settled on the lawn and I was sent to fetch Sandy's binoculars, I wished it would fly away. Couldn't I be myself?

Sandy's extra years at Cambridge were spent turning him-self into a complete naturalist. What science he cared to read was in the literary classics, taking him beyond the range of most young men, and as well as a diary he wrote vivid letters to friends who kept them. The gift of words, not so rare in a generation raised on English literature, was as precious as the art of scientific quest.

In the summers of 1896 and 1897 he went with a friend to Lapland, travelling by boat or pony cart or on foot far beyond the arctic circle. It was tough going, dossing where they could, sleeping on reindeer skins, shooting a duck or catching a trout to supplement the jaw-breaking ryebread and sour milk; and always on the lookout for birds – a pair of Siberian jays, a three-toed woodpecker. Lying by a river with *Paradise Lost* Sandy was distracted by his first merlin. He noted a cuckoo being fostered by a willow wren, he swam in a lake where an osprey was fishing, he stumbled on a rare viper, he walked through swarms of Camberwell beauty butterflies to add to his collection. Though the country was bleak, thinly inhabited, Sandy saw beauty in the vastness and the morning and evening light on trees and water: 'When you stand on a hill you see enormous stretches of forests and lakes and rivers. Lovely colours and such a clear blue sky, not like the deep Italian sky, but one you can see through to the Beyond.'

The Beyond was what drew him – more than ever after wading through swamps of mud and moss, plagued by mosquitoes: 'I have a hazy idea now of what a tropical forest must be like.' He was absorbing the skills for which another explorer was to call him 'the most aware man I have known'. But it wasn't only birds and bugs that caught his eye. Living among Lapps he watched a man pick out a hind from a herd of reindeer and lasso it by the horns for another man to milk it. He admired the foresters manoeuvring a log-jam in a river, casually smoking cigars, singing a strange chant while they hopped and balanced on the logs. And he joined a gang of men in a feast to celebrate a new telegraph line, a drunken party in a land where the sun never set.

At midnight in the most northerly port of Finnmark he saw

the captain of Nansen's arctic ship *Fram* going on board, and noted, 'He starts for Spitzbergen in the morning. Lucky dog – wish I were going too.' Without leaving Europe Sandy had tasted the struggle and joy of travel in wild country, and was hooked.

*

In 1898, having decided on an explorer's life and his best hope of joining an expedition was to equip himself with a profession, he enrolled as a student at the London Hospital in Whitechapel. But he never guessed how little he was to enjoy the work.

'Medical practice as a livelihood,' he told his father, 'does not attract me – in fact I dislike it all extremely.' And years later, after trying to dissuade a young man from becoming a doctor, he wrote hastily, 'I don't know whether he thought I was serious – perhaps not, in that case no harm was done – but sometimes a remark of that sort sticks unexpectedly and works as an active poison. I should be exceedingly sorry if that happened in this case. I made such a horrible mistake when I went in for a profession I loathe, and am so constantly regretting it, that I can't resist saying nasty things about it. To do so argues me a fool, no doubt, but I am content to risk it so long as I don't hurt another person's feelings... I am altogether a mistake – a very angular peg looking for a suitable hole, and not responsible for my words.'

During five years' study he escaped from London at the

least chance, and was soon back for a weekend at King's: 'Ate lotus. Very jolly to see so many nice people again – even nicer than before… It would be intolerable if I didn't get away sometimes, to the Saturday Pops and such good things. The Zoo would be a blessing, but it is generally dark before I can go.' In the spring a kingfisher flying over the Serpentine was a small joy, but in his lodgings in Bethnal Green it was, 'Hospital all day. Fog just thin enough to see that the sun is shining everywhere except in this cursed place. Ye gods, how I hate London!'

Packing a rucksack to hike across the beloved West Country would sustain him for more drudgery. Once he took medical books, also George Borrow's gypsy romance *Lavengro*, to a pub on the Devon coast, but spent the evenings talking to the landlord, 'the best-read man of his kind I have come across. Quotes Shakespeare, Longfellow, Ruskin, Swift, and knows Kingsley by heart. This is a place to come to every year. Never shall I forget the great gale we had soon after I came. Ships foundered along the coast and piles of wreckage have been washed ashore at every tide – masts, sails, barrels of lard and oil, ships' boats and lifebuoys. It almost makes one hate this cruel sea in spite of its beauty. Yet today it is a serene blue, as beautiful as ever – not a sign of the storm devil lurking below.'

He wangled a month at Cambridge to work at physiology, but 'spent a lot of time looking for birds.' He went to the fens for a short-eared owl's nest, and elsewhere for nightjars, peewits, Kentish plover, a turnstone. Instinctively he found what he was looking for and often something extra as bonus – a golden oriole or a pair of hares fighting in a cloud of fur. Soon he was back in the West on a bicycle, revelling in the names of 'the good old country' – Chibbet, Heddensmouth, Challacombe, Simonsbath, Muddicombe... He stopped at the same pub, sitting outside one summer evening with the landlord who next morning refused to give him a bill: 'He is quite a mystery – I never heard of an innkeeper doing that sort of thing.' After a long walk along the coast he noted, 'A gorgeous day from beginning to end. Sat out on the quay and talked Kipling with a coastguard.'

In 1899 during the Boer War, impatient for a wider, more exciting, world he volunteered for the army, only to fail the medical exam. But in the summer a friend rescued him from the hospital and in the mountains of Skye introduced him to climbing. Sandy was never an athlete and though they did some difficult rock ascents he was happier on long traverses of corries and ridges, bathing in lonely lochs, noting golden eagles and ravens; and bug-hunting – 'some nice-looking larvae of I don't know what' to be hatched at home. In the little hotel they met a veteran mountaineer who taught Sandy something of mapping. Also a Himalayan explorer with his Gurkha sergeant, a small wiry man who carried a huge rucksack barefoot over the harsh mountains and after supper astonished them with tricks – chopping pennies in half with his kukri or turning himself inside out. Sandy's imagination was drifting to new horizons, beyond these British Isles.

In the winter he was off to Devon for peregrines and a shore lark, and a freezing bathe in the sea, and to Cornwall for a tremendous moonlight walk over the cliffs. 'Sometimes I think I am horribly selfish, enjoying myself so intensely when I get into the country. It is that old lotus-eating feeling, but I wouldn't part with it for the world.' And he remembered Wordsworth:

> *So be it when I shall grow old,*
> *Or let me die!*

Back in hospital he asked himself what it was leading to. The prospect was dubious in the extreme. He was offered a job as secretary of an inquiry into the herbaria at South Kensington and Kew but rejected it as uncongenial, then wondered if he had done the right thing. The dilemma increased on hearing from a friend in Sudan, collecting for Charles Rothschild's private natural history museum: 'Lucky dogs. Confound it, why must I stay bottled up in this cursed London? Many times a week I would rush away if I had the means. Lucky perhaps that I have not got 'em, as I am really keen about this medical business and mean to go through with it – London or no London.' Replying to his friend he wrote, 'I think of sun, clear sky, roasting heat, beard-ed Arabs, wheatears, shrikes and ducks. Then I look out of the window and see gaslamps, fog, rain and mud, Arabs of the street and smutty sparrows... Nothing happens except that I get older and my temper gets worse.'

But London couldn't hold him for long. Before the end of winter he was climbing in the Lake District, cutting steps with an ice axe, tackling the hardest climbs he had done: 'A splendid holiday and a great increase in my knowledge of mountaineering.' Then off to Essex: 'Glorious day, blazing sun. Sat on many gates and enjoyed myself hugely. Gossiped with many natives – nice people all.' Then to the Chilterns for the prettiest nest he had seen, a pochard's under a gorse bush. And to Sutherland for greenshanks and golden plover. And back to Cumberland for a dotterel. And to the Skerries off Anglesey where, through wheeling flocks of seabirds, a lighthouse-keeper pointed out the roseate terns that Sandy was after. And across to Ireland to look for red-necked phalaropes and where, on a beach, he heard a curious croak and smelt something peculiar, and lifting the stones he found a pair of stormy petrels.

It's a wonder that any medical work was done at all.

*

In the summer of 1900 Sandy went with a friend to the Dolomites. They reached the mountains in pelting rain and ran to the first inn, 'an old-fashioned place with stables on the ground floor and a nice horsy smell in our bedroom. Outside there was a good smell of wet earth, wet pine trees and cows, and I knew we had got to the real beginning of our journey.' Soon they were in a bar lit by candles guttering through the smoke, crowded with people dancing among tables and barrels to a three-piece band – a player passing his accordion or horn or piccolo to the next man when he got thirsty. It was as memorable as the dawn start next morning, trudging up a glacier as the sun rose.

In the next weeks they climbed some of those spectacular peaks. But to Sandy, just being in mountain country was more precious than reaching a summit. He cared less for the huts heaving with raucous tourists and their guides among wafts of pea soup and wet clothes, than for a village inn where two priests with a dozen men and women round a table drank wine and sang in harmony: 'It was a concert one would go a good way to hear in England, and they were just a collection of peasants who chanced to be in the inn together and sang to pass the time.' Though far from frivolous – in fact a serious scientist all his life – he never missed the sensuous pleasure of wherever he happened to be; and found in the Dolomites that it was the idle days between climbs when he was happiest.

A forest with nutcrackers chattering in the pine tops, a bathe in an icy lake, a bask in the sun to smoke a pipe, a discussion with an ox-driver about his curious hay cart, a meadow of poppies and gentians, another bathe, a coffee in the market place, a storm that brought dozens of black-and-yellow salamanders out of hiding, a rainbow framing the peaks at sunset, a supper of trout and omelette – these were as wonderful as the awesome cliffs. One morning, deciding it was too hot for climbing, filling their pockets with figs and choco-late, the two young men dawdled over mountain slopes white with edelweiss and were confronted by 'a stupendous rock spire eight hunded feet high, looking perpendicular if not overhanging, as if a gust of wind would blow it into the valley below'. It was unthinkable not to stop and gaze, and while they did so a party of Germans sweltering under huge ruck-sacks came up the path, never lifting their eyes to the view, plodding upwards to their lunch.

*

Next winter Sandy was off to Sudan with Charles Rothschild to collect for the museum. On the way out he 'made a few pleasant acquaintances – as usual all of the male sex. It grew warmer and southerner and I forgot Whitechapel and all its works and became a new man. At Port Said, what with flamin-gos and pelicans, not to mention the sun and the desert, I nearly went off my head. Everything is new and wonderful, and I wander the streets and stare like a babe open-mouthed at Arabs and Turks and Copts and Nubians and mosques and kites and camels and donkeys – you can imagine my state of mind.'

In the tropics for the first time, camped by the Nile among unimagined birds and beasts, Sandy was in raptures: 'I am tremendously fit, almost as black as an Arab and as tough as possible... We live and sleep out of doors and except from twelve to three, when it is too hot to move, never feel slack.'

The snag was, there was so much to be collected: sunbirds, hornbills, bee-eaters and 'all sorts of other jolly things, possibly one or two that are new'. There was a chestnut-capped swallow breeding in the mud banks and a rare swift among the palm leaves and a little-eared owl: 'I shot the male and found the nest with two young birds. I go tomorrow to photograph them and hope to shoot the female.'

A century later his account of those months reads like a catalogue of slaughter; of wildlife shot or trapped, skinned and described and labelled, packed and shipped to England for a rich collector's pleasure. Science was pushed forward a little, nature retreated. Those irresistible birds – the brilliant barbet, the fantail warbler, the racket-tailed roller: do they survive where they had lived since the beginning of time? Or are they now perched in a mock-up setting behind glass if not lying in a drawer, limp, moth-eaten, faded, to be wondered at by some-one who can only guess at their true habitat?

Sandy's letters evoke a vast tapestry of life and I wonder how much still exists, or is there drab silence in Sudan, never a flash of purple wing or scarlet crest? His joy in the Nile valley, having native hunters bring him a snake or hedgehog, or rid-ing a camel into the desert for gazelles, is hard to share when the purpose was to kill a creature of the living world – a world beating about him as he wrote: '10 p.m. and a great flight of cranes is going over, making the devil of a noise. Spur-wing plovers whistling all round and Egyptian geese honking.'

It was a jolly life, 'better than one will ever have again', but no preparation for more years of study: 'I wish I could find some berth out here. It will be vile going back.' The whistling and honking of London would be a poor exchange.

*

Back in his lodgings, at work all day in hospital, he was invited to join an expedition to Peru or Java. Though very tempting it would mean chucking up medicine. And in 1903, through hard slog between absences, he qualified as surgeon-physician. He was 28, a doctor with an aversion to doctoring, and the future was cloudy: 'I can't for the life of me see that brass plate looming,' he told his father.

He was saved by Charles Rothschild who asked him back to Sudan; and for a year he pursued the life of a collector, forgetting – or not caring to remember – that he now had another profession. In Cairo he called on the chief of the sanitary department with a view to a job one day, a gesture of earnestness, but the chance was remote and he was thankful to be a wandering naturalist travelling upriver to Wadi Halfa – and beyond.

Birds were again the prey – in the heat they had to be skinned as soon as shot – and Sandy was pleased to find, under a stone on an island in the Nile, the nest and eggs of a desert bullfinch, something never seen before. Another delight was sitting in a tree over the river and watching a kingfisher catch a big fish, toss it in the air and snatch it several times to soften it for swallowing. For days they trekked on camels across the desert to a godforsaken place where there were wild asses, but couldn't get close enough for a shot till Rothschild gave his gun to a native hunter who stalked the herd and killed a fine male. At the thought of baksheesh the hunter broke into wild Nubian songs and in the evening Sandy went out to see the prize, amused to be walking four miles to look at a dead donkey by moonlight.

He didn't take to the fellahin, 'a lazy lot of scoundrels' whom he had to kick awake at dawn. And Rothschild, more squeamish, was horrified to learn that a crocodile's penis was preserved in honey as an aphrodisiac and virgins were sewn up to ensure their virtue. But camp life was very pleasant, sleeping under the stars, bathing in the Nile. And the diet of dates and tinned sardines was wonderfully improved when they found an English aristocrat on safari: 'We called on him and got an excellent dinner and still more excellent lager beer.'

A good collector, it was said, had a magic touch that turned a scientist into an artist, and Sandy and Rothschild went about it differently. Sandy was the budding explorer, future climber of virgin peaks, crosser of rivers, trail-blazer through jungles, delighting in risk, fired by a love of nature. Rothschild was far from tough, given to depressions and bad nerves but a meticulous zoologist, a master of detail. He called Sandy 'the Bear' because of his early morning prickliness, and claimed to be the only friend Sandy had never quarrelled with before breakfast. Between the two there was often friction and Sandy wrote to a friend who had passed on a remark: 'You might tell Rothschild that he erred greatly when he said I could probably make myself very unpleasant if I wanted. I have sometimes tried when people irked me badly, and failed miserably. I only wish I could.'

Together, Jewish millionaire and impecunious doctor, they hit it off: Sandy depending on Rothschild's patronage and the chance to travel, Rothschild valuing Sandy's no-nonsense ways, his lack of bluff or swagger. Several times in later life Sandy's frankness was to save his friend from an attack of the blues. And when Rothschild spent two desperate years in Switzerland after his health collapsed Sandy diagnosed the trouble as schizophrenia – a harsh though candid verdict that Rothschild counted as real friendship. Sadly for me, they agreed to destroy each other's letters on getting married. Something was lost that might have been revealing about two unusual young men.

At the end of the expedition, after jogging for days over the roasting desert on a camel, Sandy was thankful for the luxury of the Sudan railway; though less so, back in Cairo, when they 'assumed the order of the boiled shirt and collar after three months of flannel shirt and comfort.' But Rothschild was delighted with the trip: 'We bagged six hundred mammals and birds, five hundred fleas and a fair lot of beetles and butterflies.' New species were named after expedition members but their best find, the plague-carrying flea, was honoured in memory of the Pharaoh Cheops of the third millenium B.C.

*

'I am going East to catch bugs for Charles Rothschild,' Sandy wrote from Egypt to a sister, and soon was on his way.

It meant postponement of a solid job and this hand-to-mouth life wasn't ideal. Private doctor to some globe-trotting invalid could be the answer, but there wasn't one in sight. And while the Russo-Japanese war was raging he might get taken on in a military hospital. But at the moment, steaming across the Indian Ocean, he was losing his heart to another passenger, a girl of fifteen who tried to teach him to dance: 'If only she had three or four of my years, what an opportunity it would be!' Another kind of wistfulness gripped him in Colombo where he caught the real smell of the East, 'enough to make me wish for more'. But he failed to trap an albatross that followed the ship and though the girl gave him more dancing lessons he was in a 'devilish temper all day'.

Nor did he care for his brief sight of Australia. Fremantle he dismissed as 'a more one-horse forsaken town I was seldom in – three-quarters of the houses are bars.' And though Melbourne was saved by laughing jackasses in the trees and a jolly evening with the chief customs officer, Wollaston by name and a distant relative, Sydney under a cloud of smoke was 'a beastly place with dirty shoddy buildings'. In Sandy's view Falmouth harbour was just as fine and Fowey infinitely prettier. He took refuge in the botanical gardens and the art gallery, but the pictures were 'fearful rubbish' or 'villainous copies of old masters'. Cities didn't agree with him, he ached for the wild places of the world.

Reprieve came with a Cambridge man, also from King's, and together they celebrated Sandy's birthday in a true Australian way. By tram and ferry they went to the far reaches of Sydney harbour where they hired a boat and rowed up a creek to make a campfire: 'The smell of burning gum leaves was new to me and I shall never forget it.' They boiled a billy-can for tea and ate an ox-tongue with bread and apples, and though it rained most of the time they sheltered under a sail and Sandy was happy at last. Three miles from the city, but for all the signs of man they might have been with Captain Cook. When the rain stopped they stalked through the bush, another first for Sandy, with huge gum trees and flowering shrubs to delight him. All that was missing were birds – only two and both were silent.

Bird life was better in New Zealand, thrushes and larks and finches in full song among familiar trees and hedges – he could hardly believe it wasn't an autumn evening in England. The hills were good hunting-ground for the Rothschild museum, but for such an un-urban traveller the cities – 'all towns are cities here' – were dirty little places full of young men loafing at street corners. Somehow he nosed out another Wollaston, a museum curator, 'not the least bit of a fossil', and in Tasmania he was asked to dinner by a Kingsman and his family. The lady sang Schubert and Schumann all evening, a pleasure hardly diminished when Sandy was dragged to the piano to render Widecombe Fair. It seems that local people, unless utter savages and thus fit for scientific study, were interesting only if there was some affinity of kin or kindred.

On the Rothschild payroll he voyaged by coastal steamer or schooner from Australia to New Britain and the Bismarck archipelago, then along the coast of New Guinea and through the Dutch East Indies, finally to Japan. In small ports and trading stations he landed with his net and collecting boxes, tramping through villages and plantations, sometimes deep into the forest where butterflies were abundant but often inaccessible. A beautiful specimen sunning itself on a treetop had to be left there, never to be killed and pinned into a glass case, but hundreds were dispatched to England.

Forty years later, in a minesweeper at the end of the Second World War, I sailed those seas, wondering at the patterns traced by father and son. I even tried to get demobilized there, dreaming of being mate on one of the small cargo boats that plied the archipelago, ending up as an old sea dog sipping a sundowner in some aromatic harbour.

A scientist… But Sandy was alert to the beautiful, the strange, the distracting. He could appreciate a little harbour with houses built over the water and an old Portuguese fort above, and be appalled by another of bamboo shanties reeking of sewage and half-dried fish. He was unimpressed by a visit to a Malay raja, a scallywag in dirty clothes and bare feet, his teeth black with betel juice, squatting in a hut under posters for beer and brandy; but in the marketplace he was enthralled by a crowd of gamblers round a cockfight. Though he went to look at the temples of Borobudur, the view over plains and mountains was better than the unending carvings of Buddha. Worst of all were the zoo and botanical gardens of Java: 'Full of bars and bandstands – not a bird or beast in the place and no more than a dozen kinds of trees, none of them labelled.' And the local food! 'Tiffin here vile, only relieved by mangosteens, an excellent fruit with an elusive taste.'

He was tired of this itinerant employment, itching for a real explorer's life. The world and its strange people were being probed, deserts traversed, mountain ranges penetrated. First ascents had been made in the Caucasus, the Andes, the Himalayas. The poles would soon be reached. After the empire-builders, who had more or less done their job, it was time for the discoverers. And for a naturalist there were untold treasures to be revealed in the certainty that nobody had seen them before.

*

Meanwhile in Japan there was adventure ready-made if Sandy could get near the fighting, and though he was sorry no

Russian warship stopped his steamer entering Nagasaki it at least had to be escorted through minefields. He had to undergo a 'very particular' medical inspection by five doctors before being allowed ashore, then was caught up in celebrations of a victory over the Russians, everyone carrying flags or paper lanterns, the whole place decked in red and white, 'better than any street decorations in England'. He hoped to find someone to give him a pass into the war zone, but it looked unlikely.

In a town famous for its potteries he was entranced: 'I could watch all day a man take a lump of clay, spin the wheel with a touch of his foot, then by magic conjure a beautiful saki flask.' But in a Japanese inn without chairs or tables his bones ached, and he was barely amused when four 'maidens' brought him tea and helped him drink it, with chatter and giggles over his efforts from a phrase book: 'They are quite engaging after a sort of kittenish style, but to my mind more ugly than pretty.' He was still less at ease in a bath-house where naked men and women and children strolled about in a way shocking to an Englishman. When he was in his bath and a woman came to join him, he grabbed a towel and fled.

Strictly these were no longer Victorian times but attitudes lingered, not least towards the peculiar habits of foreigners. A generation later Sandy's son, I may say, wouldn't have been so restrained. And at about the same age, travelling through Persia, I wallowed happily in a public steam bath, to the rattle of buckets and clanging of bells, the distant whiff of opium, the cleansing slap of flesh: a curiosity to other bathers who had never before seen freckles on a man's back and watched keenly while an attendant with a special abrasive glove tried to scrape them off.

Sandy had no qualms about the sinewy coolies who pulled his rickshaw day after blazing day, sweating a thousand feet into the hills, bowling back to the coast. It was the way to travel, and the roadside was a mass of flowers and trees he had never seen. Enchantment was almost too much on a sacred island famous for its Shinto shrine, where no carts or rickshaws or dogs were allowed, or even births or burials. Sandy had to stop every yard to look at a pretty house, a temple, a view of water. Wild deer came down to the shore to take food from his hand, but the greatest glory was in the pines of every kind and maples breaking into autumn colour, tended reverently by the people. It hardly mattered that they collected round, drawn by his height and features and fair hair, to stare at such a strange being.

The Russo-Japanese war loomed closer but Sandy couldn't get there. Somehow, brandishing his medical degree, he fixed an introduction to an American woman doctor superintending hospitals in Hiroshima – 'this is just what I wanted' – and took a sampan over the water to meet her. Soldiers and horses and wagons swarmed through the town, with sentries at street corners and recruits in the barracks learning to march and bugle.

In a hospital so full of wounded that hundreds more were housed in stables and temples, Sandy was impressed by the men's pluck. Only among the worst cases, wretched beyond recovery, did he find the solemnity of an English ward. Otherwise it was all jokes and laughter: 'One fellow with holes through his head and belly gave me a graphic description of how the bullets came, with appropriate sounds... I didn't hear a cry or groan... I think they feel pain every bit as much as Europeans, but it is a point of honour to hide it.'

Perhaps his sympathy with Russia over Japan had to be revised. Certainly the doctor who gave up her morning for him healed one blind spot: 'Though I have never met a woman doctor before and am not a little prejudiced against them, I shall have to alter my opinions a bit. She told me a lot of interesting things.' A century later I wonder what Sandy would have thought of his own granddaughter, a highly qualified general practitioner in London.

Failing to get near the war he sailed to Vancouver and stayed with his brother on a ranch in British Columbia. There were duck and prairie chicken to shoot, and he 'vastly' enjoyed his attempt at horse-riding, galloping over the country in a paperchase. Best of all there were 'heaps of nice people, all most hospitable, and in one month I went into more houses than in London in a year.' Those far-flung colonials had no problem melting a shy young Englishman's inhibitions. By the end of 1904 he was back in London and went straight to a concert in the Queen's Hall.

Though he had been round the world and packed off hundreds of specimens – many rare, some unknown – to the Rothschild museum, later absorbed into the British Museum, he had gazed on no new lands, trodden no fresh peaks, explored nowhere except perhaps into himself. In tiny writing he had pencilled thoughts and comments into a diary and written letters home. But he was a man of his time and class – phlegmatic, prejudiced, reluctant to give much away – and it's hard to get a view of such an innocent abroad, intelligent, reserved, alone in an exotic world. Did he ever unburden himself of all the stuff he never noted down? Did even Mary, the woman he married twenty years later, read between the lines or pick his memory to fill the gaps? Or was he bottled up, divulging nothing to the end?

As his son, more than seventy years after his death, I still don't know the answers.

II RUWENZORI

'I am seriously alarmed about myself,' Sandy confessed to a friend in 1905. 'Often I wish I had never been out of England, for the more I wander the less inclined I am to stay at home. A year ago I thought I had come back for good, but at the first chance I threw up the work I had and was off. I have a notion that unless a man has fixed himself up in his round or square hole by thirty-five he never will, and I haven't much time left. The worst is that I have no money and this sort of thing does not pay.'

Finding nobody to employ him as an explorer, he had taken a job as house surgeon at Addenbrooke's Hospital in Cambridge. It was his first medical post and being five minutes from King's College as congenial as he could hope for. But two days after starting, barely resigned to 'the awful prospect of hospital life', he heard of a scientific expedition from the British Museum to the Ruwenzori mountains on the borders of Uganda and the Belgian Congo. The other members had already sailed but they were short of a botanist, an entomologist and a doctor. Sandy was all three. He dashed to London, fixed it up, found a substitute for the hospital and got away with a fortnight to prepare for a year in Africa. He was to be paid £12 a month.

Slow boat to Mombasa, the new railway through Kenya to Lake Victoria, a steamer to Entebbe and rickshaw to Kampala, two weeks' march to Fort Portal, another week up into the Ruwenzori with delays to hire porters and sort baggage – it was three months before he joined the expedition in the mountains. But tough as he was, and driven by a passion to explore, he never missed the beauty of the scene he passed through. Across the Kenya plains by train, while other passengers were gasping at the herds of game and swapping tales of man-eating lions, it was the huge snow cone of Kilimanjaro shimmering a hundred miles away that stirred Sandy. The view from the escarpment before plunging into the Great Rift Valley bowled him over. And he stopped for some days to camp on an island in the lovely Lake Naivasha, revelling in its birds and plants, trying to evoke its mystery in words: 'It is said of the blessed of one nation that when they die they go to Paris. To others life is complete when they have seen Naples. For my part, had I never seen those cities, I should have been content when I had seen Naivasha.'

From the British government post at Entebbe, where cricket and tennis seemed to be the rule, he was thankful to escape into the wilderness. Now he was alone, tramping through Africa at the head of thirty porters. With only enough Swahili to call a man the offspring of a snake, he was given some phrases in dialect by a missionary which had a magic effect on his porters. Along the way he picked up tips for a journey that in the end would take him across the continent, coast to coast.

Start the day's march before dawn, he learnt, to catch the sunrise when each leaf and blade of grass glitters with dew, mist rises from the swamps and the air is filled with birdsong; otherwise, when the sun is up and a great fatigue falls on the land, the porters halt under every tree. Walk at a distance from them – 'I shall never come to tolerate the peculiar bouquet of the African' – and carry an umbrella, to stay in the shade in dry weather and partly dry in the rain; though later, lashing into a gang of porters armed with spears and eating stolen bananas, 'truculent-looking ruffians but arrant cowards where a white man is concerned', he broke his umbrella on a black man's head. Overfamiliarity with local women must be punished but use of the stick, which is expected and preferred to a cut in pay, leads to trouble. But with adequate food and tobacco, hard work and rest days, there are no problems. A good 'boy' has a fire going to make tea while the tents are being pitched. A hot bath or sponge-down every evening is vital; also regular bowels ensured by porridge for breakfast and a nightly dose of 'Livingstone Rouser'. And a lonely Christmas dinner in camp – dehydrated soup, curried chicken, lukewarm pudding from a tin – can be transformed by a waterlily stuck in a bottle on the table and, after raising a glass of lager to friends and family at home, a pipe of tobacco and bed with the faithful Samuel Pepys.

For four months, in the foothills between the grilling plains and alpine snows, the expedition collected fauna and flora. These mad white men, the natives found, would pay for any creatures brought to them – worms and snakes, beetles, rats and mice, chameleons, hyraxes. Traps were set for something bigger, but caught only a small girl held by the foot, screaming. Her parents dressed the wound with an 'unspeakable mixture' which made it worse, and she became Sandy's only patient. But his medical career, aborted at Cambridge, drifted gently on in the forest. There were jiggers to be extracted, fevers – real or not – to be calmed, malingerers to be sent packing with a purgative: 'A black man is always sick if there's a chance of getting medicine. They consume huge doses of even the nastiest.' The expedition gramophone was also popular, especially a song about Jerusalem and choirboys.

None of the others were climbers, but Sandy's heart was in the mountains: 'I am consumed with desire to be up and doing.' The few Europeans ever to reach the glaciers had been beaten by the appalling weather. The peaks remained unknown and mysterious – a challenge waiting under a pall of cloud. Sandy badly wanted to make the first ascent. Then to his anguish the dream was shattered at a blow. The Duke of the Abruzzi, brother of the king of Italy and an illustrious mountaineer, was on his way with a vast expedition to explore the range: 'He will be at the top of the highest peak before I get within fifty miles... I am inclined to curse all royal dukes and wish they would stop at home.'

Meanwhile it was the rare view of landscape, seen or hoped for, that saved him from monotony: trudging along tracks hedged by dense grass where nothing was visible but the back of the man in front, or groping through tunnels of forest. But 'anyone who loves walking in a wood knows how hard it is to turn back. There is always something further – a turn in the path, a stream to cross, an enticing hill beyond.' All his life that never-never land, the elusive Beyond, was the goal. And here Sandy was lured on by an antelope leaping from his feet, a tribe of monkeys swinging through the branches: 'Sunbeams reaching the ground, mysterious shadows and the desire to see a little more, beckoned one from tree to tree.' Then a glint of light showed ahead, the forest ended, a panorama opened up – the more rewarding if the clouds rolled away for a moment to reveal the delectable mountains.

'I tear my hair,' he wrote to a friend at home, 'when I look up at all these peaks and valleys that no one has even peeped into… You have an English spring and strawberries by the time this reaches you, whilst I am a rotten old ne'erdoweel starving on goat and bananas – heavens! how sick of them I am… I wish I were a Bateleur eagle – there is one flying over the camp now. Hawthorn and dog roses – it's the only time of year that I get homesick.'

At last, under cover of collecting specimens, Sandy led a small party up towards the snows. Soon they were drenched to the skin, plunging into mud and bracken, cutting through bamboo, losing their bearings in the mist. On a soggy patch under cascades of water from a cliff they laid out their bedding, to find that after dark the place echoed with mournful cries and bloodcurdling shrieks – whether uttered by frogs or owls or devils they never learnt. Next day's climb was no less a torment: swamps strewn with decayed trees that crumbled at a touch, draped with cushions of moss, beards of lichen. Higher, they reached a tract of near-prehistoric aspect where pterodactyls might scream and iguanadons flounder, though the silence and solitude were awful. And for another night, huddled by a fire of sodden logs, they camped under rocks haunted by giant fruit-bats where any chance of sleep, troubled enough by leopard tracks nearby, was dashed by an earthquake.

During their days in that unearthly place the mountains showed for only a few hours, but there were plants to discover and a gorgeous sunbird, dark metallic green shot with iridescent purple. Then one dawn the peak that Sandy had his eye on appeared in a parting of the clouds, and before it vanished he marked a possible route. Natural history was dropped, the British Museum was far away, and with one companion he started for the snows. At such altitude any exertion was a labour and soon they abandoned their cameras and spare food. Vegetation thinned out, moss and mud gave way to rock; but when they reached a granite wall, clouds had swept over everything; they had to grope blindly upwards. Remembering Hansel and Gretel they scattered a trail of flowers to be sure of finding the way back; and climbed over steep rocks, up a glacier with increasing snow, thicker cloud, till a dark mass loomed ahead. And seven hours after leaving camp they stood on the summit.

They built a cairn and to keep warm or announce the conquest of Ruwenzori hurled rocks down into the valley. But they got no view till starting to descend, when clouds boiled up from below and in a piercing slant of sunshine the plains of Uganda were revealed far to the east. Another window opened to the west 'and we saw that we had missed the real top of our mountain, which rose a hundred and fifty feet higher, joined by an arête of snow. It was disappointing, but too late to go on.' With one ice axe between them and a piece of rope too short for any use, wandering in fog along an unknown ridge with invisible slopes on either side would be madness. It was enough to have got higher than anyone, to nearly 16,000 feet, and reached the watershed.

A month later with two companions Sandy climbed another peak, but after waiting hours for the clouds to break they had to retreat, sorry and bedraggled. Next day Sandy stayed in his tent, dodging the water that fell from above and reading *Don Quixote*; perhaps reflecting too poignantly on the deluded knight's adventures. Ruwenzori kept its secrets but on the far side, westward towards the Congo, there were higher mountains to be explored.

The Beyond was always there.

*

The Duke of the Abruzzi, hoping for useful tips on Ruwenzori, invited the British expedition to meet him at Fort Portal. It meant a sixty-mile walk each way along a hot and thirsty road, but after months of camp life Sandy would have gone there for 'even a less interesting personage than the distinguished Italian explorer'. In a baggage train four hundred strong the duke had a doctor, geologist, photographer, two Alpine guides and four Swiss porters, equipped for a grand assault. The local African king, saluting royal blood, turned out to greet them with his private band; also missionaries sweating in suits and dog-collars and pale ladies on bicycles – the biggest crowd of Europeans ever seen.

Sandy got on well with the duke, 'lean and tough... a climber by the look of him', and passed on what he knew about Ruwenzori: the lie of the glaciers and ridges, the likely routes. But he confessed to a pang of envy when the huge party, bound for conquest, disappeared into the mountains: 'I wish they had not come this year as I should dearly like to have been first on the highest peak.' Over the next weeks, when the weather was tantalizingly fine, he watched the mountains adazzle in the sun and told himself they were in the best possible hands – those of an aristocrat of exploration though sadly not an Englishman: 'If he can get a tent on to the upper snows all will be plain sailing.' It was heartbreaking but no surprise that the duke mapped the whole range and climbed the major peaks. Some of them he named after Italian royalty, others after earlier explorers. Courteously, repaying Sandy's help, he called one Wollaston Peak.

Sandy was only mildly flattered. He favoured 'good native names', however unwieldy. Why should an obscure point in geography commemorate the obscure man who first thought of going there? To him the joy of discovery was greater than the honour of his name on the map. Not that he expected many others to follow in his tracks. The long march to the foothills – with elephant grass 'hitting you in the face, knocking your hat off, pulling your pipe out of your mouth until you wonder why you were ever fool enough to leave home' – would deter most climbers. And any who reached the mountains, as well as the risk of seeing nothing at the end, faced the daily struggle to rouse the porters at dawn and coax life into the fire for a joyless breakfast before plunging into a morass, soaked through in fifty yards.

To Sandy the fascination of an unknown world and the strangely beautiful scenery made up for the trials. Even the forest's quiet gloom held a curious allure: 'To feel it properly you must walk a mile or two behind your caravan, or better, sit out at sundown and hear the day-things go to bed and the night-things come out.' If he got another chance of falling into a moss-covered mud-trap or being tripped by a wandering root or hearing the thud of rain and rattle of foliage in a squall, he wouldn't hesitate. And there was plenty to keep an explorer happy, the wilderness was still inviolate. Fixed ropes and pitons had not yet appeared, the empty sardine tin and broken bottle were strangers in the land – 'and long may they continue to be so.'

Sandy in his thirties

The British expedition's work in eastern Ruwenzori was finished; they moved to the west before making a circuit of the range and back to Fort Portal. Coming down to the plains from the forest, where any horizon was hidden in clouds or vegetation, was like being let out of prison. Suddenly there was the great African sky, a wonder by day or night with thunderstorms flickering far away, and firm ground underfoot and acacias in blossom, white and scented like hawthorn. Given a windmill or two and a distant church Sandy could imagine himself in England: a fine rest cure after so long in the mountains. But there had to be a catch. Equatorial heat wasn't enough; they were beset by ticks, mosquitoes, lions, disagreeable natives banging their terrible drums. Luckily there was a lake close by, beloved of hippos. Sandy would watch them at play, snorting, splashing, gambolling, and saw in them something irresistibly human. Only bathing-huts were missing. Later he discovered that hippo fillet was not bad eating – anyway in Africa.

The first attempt to cross into Belgian territory was a disaster: the boundary river was a rushing torrent. But in time – lethargic African time – with bits of box-cord tied into a rope and 'a tatterdemalion collection of natives' the baggage was ferried to the other side. Sandy tried to follow, only to be swept downstream when the rope broke. Fished out half-drowned, he stripped off to swim across a pool where the current was easier, and on the far bank introduced himself to the officer of the frontier post: a dripping, blushing Englishman dressed in only a sun helmet and a lieutenant of the Belgian grenadiers in spotless white uniform. Champagne was broached, a merry evening was spent, the host sacrificed his bed to the visitor and next morning, roused by a smart black bugler, Sandy had a genial view of King Leopold's private colony.

It was not to last. Unruly tribes in the mountains were making trouble, the expedition wasn't allowed beyond the garrison fort unless escorted by a Belgian sergeant and thirty native soldiers. On its own, Sandy believed, a party of scientists with unarmed porters would be less provocative. But anything to get to grips with Ruwenzori again, and from this side, though often in their familiar clouds, the peaks rose dramatically over the forest.

Tree-heaths and giant groundsels, Ruwenzori (12,500ft)

At the sight of a military troop the natives took to the hill-tops, waving spears, shouting defiance. A few stood their ground and Sandy found it 'rather disconcerting to see one gentleman, not a dozen yards from me, taking aim with bow and arrow'. The soldiers opened fire and 'he disappeared like a shadow in the long grass.' They camped in a ripening bean-field – and wrecked it – but the people had fled, leaving an old man and woman who were secured with halters round their necks and made to join the caravan. All night yells and whistles came tearing out of the dark, with drums and war-horns, though an attack was foiled by a thunderstorm. But it was ominous for an expedition with designs on the life of nothing bigger than a butterfly. And next day it got worse. Among a cluster of huts in a banana plantation the sergeant decided to camp. His soldiers cut down the bananas which might shelter an enemy, killed the only cow, looted the huts. There was no chance for the English to make friends.

Further up, where three streams fell from the highest peaks, they set up a base. The sergeant and half his men were sent back with orders to return in two weeks – time enough to explore. Sandy and one companion, Carruthers, went on up beyond the bamboo line to a zone filled with the scent of heather and conifer. High on the western slopes they pitched tents with a thrilling view over the Congo forest in front and, behind, towering ridges and a glimpse of one snow-peak after another. 'We had hopes of climbing where no white man had set foot.' Treated to a glorious crimson sunset they began to think life was worth living – there were worse places in the world than Ruwenzori.

Curiously the promise was borne out on coming across a pair of breeches, unmistakably English. Whose were they?

What explorer had taken off his trousers and left them there? Had he gone higher or stayed to haunt the mountains? No answers came, but in an odd way it seemed an auspicious find.

Next day their hopes were shattered by a message from the lower camp. The sergeant had walked into an ambush. Losing one man killed and five wounded to a horde of natives, he had decided everyone must withdraw. To Sandy, within a few hours of the snows – 'with a chance of doing something really worthwhile' – it was cruel ill-luck. That night, while an enormous Jupiter sank in the west and a full moon rose, the peaks stood clearer than ever in 'a sky of regal splendour... to spite me, I believe'. At dawn he scrambled higher for a view of the snows but the clouds were down; he turned sadly to the turmoil below.

There were wounds to be bandaged, bullets to be gouged out. And retreat down the valley became a three-day running fight. Carrying the wounded in hammocks, also the dead soldier for burial at home – rotting in the heat, minus a hand hacked off for a trophy – made them dangerously slow, but 'even the extremity of fear will not prevent a black man from loitering if he can.' With simple tactics the natives could have cut the caravan to pieces but stayed hidden in the forest, hurling spears, shooting arrows. The soldiers fired blindly into the undergrowth, hitting only an elephant, and the porters gibbered with terror. Now there were wounds from poisoned arrows to be sucked out – not a branch of surgery taught in a London medical school.

Sandy was glad to reach the garrison fort, though less so when the Belgians sent a punitive force into the mountains 'to quell these wretched people'. His dream was over. The expedition had to abandon western Ruwenzori, but their collections were some of the finest seen at the British Museum, many of them new to science.

Though I have worked in Africa I never went to Ruwenzori but my daughter, trekking in her youth, saw her grandfather's peak and laughed irreverently at the sight of his lobelia thrusting an enormous phallus from the ground.

*

The members dispersed and took different routes back to England. Desperate to be home for the partridge season one of them made a dash by forced marches to Mombasa and the next boat. Hardly worth it, Sandy thought, when a man could shoot partridges any year of his life. But he surprised himself at the thrill of hunting a water buck. Though far from bloodthirsty he confessed to exultation when the long stalk, crawling behind a tuft of grass or trying to look like an acacia tree, ended in a kill; pleased also to find he could hold a rifle more or less straight. It was his first 'head', to be treasured with memories of his first trout and first snow mountain.

Another 'interview', as he called it, with big game was more sombre. He was at a Belgian post in a game reserve when a herd of elephants was reported nearby. With the officer in charge, who took a rifle 'in case of accidents', Sandy went out to look at them, but no sooner in range than the officer opened fire, blazing away wildly. Caught between a madman with a gun and a crowd of natives trying to drive them off their crops, fifty elephants stampeded. By the time the officer's ammunition ran out several were wounded, helped to escape by their companions, and one was left dead on the battlefield. Sandy was disgusted, he had seen enough elephant-shooting to last his life. But when two of the wounded were found wandering about, he went out to finish them off. At least he could sell the ivory – five pounds a tusk. And many years later an elephant's tail, a wretched dry tassel, hung on the wall of his study in our Cambridge house.

In no hurry to be home Sandy and Carruthers decided to trek across Africa to the west coast. Canoeing down Lake Albert Edward with a last view of Ruwenzori far behind was pure delight: sandbanks abounding with birds and hippos, villages built in the water to avoid the lions that preyed on huge herds of game. But then the travellers, already weakened with malaria, were attacked by tick fever. High temperature, acute pain, vomiting, diarrhoea, became a two-week nightmare of recovery and relapse. With both men prostrate they had to quit the region for somewhere healthier. Bumping and jogging in hammocks through a wonderful landscape but too ill to open their eyes, they reached a hill station where the Belgians got ready for a funeral. But with strawberries for breakfast, fresh butter and cheese, lettuces, artichokes and the magnificent Mfumbiro volcanoes to gaze at – with dreams of exploring them one day – they recovered.

Touched with patriotism, tinged with racism, Sandy compared Belgian rule in the Congo with what he had seen of the British in Kenya and Uganda. 'A passing traveller', he admitted, 'sees many things, faults and merits alike, to which the man who sees them daily is blind.' But the proper way to run a colony, after doing it for centuries, flowed like a gift of nature in British blood. And the Belgians were beginners, they had a lot to learn. Nearly every official kept a black mistress while the British, if they did the same, hid her behind a screen of respectability. Smug and hypocritical perhaps, but 'a better state of things'. Any hope of improving the native races meant keeping a distance, winning respect, and when black men saw their women being treated wantonly by their masters all was lost. A sudden burst of cruelty wasn't enough, as Sandy noted when a boy was given twenty-five lashes of the rhino-whip for breaking a cup. And what should he think of the commandant whose other guest at dinner was a chimpanzee sitting at the table, drinking soup with a spoon? 'It was a horrible caricature of humanity... I was not at all sorry when we no longer dined with Joseph.'

Reciting the maxim, 'In Africa believe nothing that you hear and only half that you see', he recovered his temper on the canoe voyage down Lake Kivu, a place itself of moods: green reflected hills cracked by squalls tearing over the water, creating a cauldron of seethe and hiss. There was no happier way of travel than to sit in the bow – 'there are excellent reasons for sitting in front of the paddlers' – and feel the surge of the canoe being driven forward. The steersman sang a recitative in high falsetto, the crew took up a chorus, rich and expressive, descending by quarter-tones to the deepest bass. The song was about Sandy and Carruthers, bawdy and unflattering.

On islands in the lake they were the first white men ever seen, prototypes with a train of porters carrying their camp furniture, but made friends on exchanging a box of matches for the natives' fire machine – a stick of hardwood, a piece of soft bamboo, a scrap of bark. Barter, they found, was ruled by fashion. They had brought fine white calico and large

Kivu native making fire

blue beads – good enough for savages, an Indian trader had said – but found that small red beads were wanted or none at all. And while one village was happy with white cloth, the next demanded blue or spotted and a third would only take brass wire.

From Lake Kivu to Lake Tanganyika they hired new porters – giants who trotted off under huge loads, reaching the next camp long before the white men: a change from the laziness, truculence, greed, they had met before. To Sandy, far from being 'our black brothers', Africans in general were an abomination, the less primitive the more boorish. He admired the noble savage more than the black man copying the white man; and could forgive nudity – men in nothing but earrings, women in beads and telegraph wire – for their splendid proportions, their glossy skin. But Europeans had had a bad

A rough sea on Tangyanyika

effect on their manners and he wrote of 'the unreasoning nature of the black mind'. It wouldn't endear him to future generations.

Into the vast Congo basin they followed an old Arab slave route. News of their journey was passed ahead, a message drummed out on a hollow piece of wood, carrying across hills and water to warn the next village. But when Carruthers' fever returned and he was too ill to walk, they came to regret the bush telegraph.

Stopping in a village for more porters to carry the hammock, faced by exorbitant demands for pay, Sandy slapped a man's face. Careless, impatient, trivial, he thought. No worse than the day when he had caught the porters loafing about in an orgy of beans and bananas and had cut the headman's spear in two: the shaft made a new handle for his butterfly net and the blade a favourite paperknife. But this time it was reported to the police and the district judge, with lurid fabrications as it went through ever grander officials to the state capital. Weeks after his crime Sandy was brought before a high court luminary, 'a person of intelligence' at last, and acquitted.

Keeping clear of politics he was drawn to lonely men trying to govern an impossible country – not quite 'a shambles swimming in blood' nor 'a negro's paradise' but something in between. A lieutenant posted to a howling tract of bush and swamp was ruler of half a dozen huts round the patch of mud where his soldiers drilled. But he had missed his vocation, he should have been a singer or, better, a gardener. Visiting his potatoes at any spare moment he laid bets in tobacco with Sandy on the yield of each plant. And sitting outside with his guest after dinner – invariably stuffed cabbage spun out with elaborate salad-making from his garden produce – he sang from his small repertoire to the listening night and wondering natives; nearly weeping for joy when Sandy joined him in *Frère Jacques*. It became a regular number in their concerts. And it saved the lieutenant from the fate of another young man whose solitude so tortured his mind that he believed a leopard hid behind every bush and his neighbours were cannibals. He never moved from his house without armed soldiers and a revolver in his pocket, and greeted Sandy and Carruthers with desperate relief.

After trudging for a month through country scourged by sleeping sickness they saw a grey streak of water ahead – a Congo tributary. Though still in the middle of Africa with another two thousand miles to the sea it felt like the end of the journey. No more stifling swamps or elephant grass, no more weary ups and downs or squabbles over porters' pay. And the district officer had newspapers less than three months old.

Now it was downstream all the way. Gliding with the current in huge canoes it was enough for the paddlers to give a lazy stroke or two for steerage way, but in a race with another canoe or heading for a place to camp they could drive the boat with tremendous force. 'Merry fellows', Sandy called them and transcribed their songs into his diary. Sitting on a chair under a little roof of leaves, watching Africa slip into the background, he felt drunk with tranquillity. There was a flock of geese on a sandbank, a crocodile, hippos dozing in a back water, a village where chickens and eggs or an elephant steak could be had. This was royal progress, each day dissolving into mystery as the trembling sun sank from the sky and a moon rose over the forest.

It was less than twenty years since the first white man, H. M. Stanley, had come this way. He wasn't sure where the river was heading – it might be the Congo or the Nile or even the Niger – he only knew it was dangerous. Villages were decorated with human skulls, fleets of canoes came out to attack, full of warriors shouting, 'Meat! Meat!' Sandy didn't doubt that cannibals still abounded, but he and Carruthers were lean of flesh, made worse by fever, and presented a frugal meal.

Further down, from Stanleyville to Leopoldville, they travelled on the upper deck of a big stern-wheeler. Sixteen days through shifting channels, stopping to load wood for the boiler, and for ivory and rubber and parrots and monkeys for Europe. At sunset the boat was moored to the bank, the bell rang for supper, the great river slid past to the throb of cicadas and bullfrogs in the forest, the rattle of a falling leaf. Probably Sandy was unaware that recently the captain of a Congo riverboat had been Joseph Conrad, one of his best-loved writers.

And he would never know that I too, nearly eighty years later, followed him down that huge inland waterway. My boat was diesel-driven, dragging five double-decker barges alongside it, rusty and leaking: a floating town of two thousand people and their animals, with shops and laundries, barbers, butchers, kitchens, a beer hall and, if not quite a brothel, a number of busy market girls. The machinery of empire had rotted in the climate, but Sandy – and Conrad – would have recognized the villages we passed, thatched and clustered by the river, and the immense green density of forest beyond. 'This stillness of life did not in the least resemble peace,' Conrad wrote. 'It was the stillness of an implacable force brooding over an inscrutable intention.' It worried him that men were living and hunting in there, somehow a threat to his own precarious confidence: 'The consciousness of there being people in that bush, so silent, so quiet... made me uneasy.'

Carruthers also felt troubled in Africa. Long afterwards, as my godfather, he taught me to sail a dinghy on the Norfolk coast. We entered a race, but he was more interested in talking about his long friendship with Sandy than in competing and I was happy to listen. But he never fell for Africa and kept away from damp, steamy country. The rest of his life he spent exploring the dry, empty deserts of Mongolia, Turkestan, Arabia.

Their African journey together ended at the mouth of the Congo. Back in London, approaching his own watershed of thirty-five years, Sandy looked for a job but didn't know what job he wanted, and settled down to write a book: 'If I had written on paper all that I have written in my head, the second-hand bookshops would be twice as full of rubbish as they are.' *From Ruwenzori to the Congo* was published in 1908. Africa was a beast, he wrote, often disagreeable, sometimes dangerous, but he had come under its spell and tried to convey 'something of the feel and smell as it appeared to me on hot and hilly roads, on winding waterways and cloud-girt mountains'. But putting it into words was nothing to the reality and paid no better: 'I really believe,' he told a friend, 'that a wife is the only thing that could keep me at home. And that for how long, I wonder? So in a year's time you may hear either that I am married or off again to Rumtifoo.'

He was off again, naturally.

III   NEW GUINEA

Smoke signals went up along the shore, a fleet of canoes came out to greet the steamer. The bigger ones were manned by twenty men standing naked, furiously wielding long paddles. The swing of their bodies, their precision and rhythm – to Sandy it was prettier than any rowing 'eight' he had seen on the river at Cambridge.

He was doctor, botanist, entomologist, of a British expedition to Dutch New Guinea: six naturalists and surveyors with a Dutch lieutenant and two sergeants, forty Javanese soldiers, sixty convicts – murderers among them, freed from their chains – and ten Gurkhas. A gang of East Indian coolies would be arriving soon. They were to map a tract of country, make natural history collections and – Sandy's recurring dream – find a way to New Guinea's backbone, the unexplored Nassau mountains. But it was a hermetic land of jungle threaded by rivers, thinly inhabited by Papuans in scattered, impermanent villages. Travellers in the past had been butchered for a feast; the country was left to stew in dark primeval stagnation. This year, 1910, enlightenment was on the march, mystery was being probed.

From the coast the view was bleak. Behind the mangrove

fringe a belt of steamy vegetation stretched back thirty miles to the first hills. Beyond, the mountains rose steeply, ridge after ridge dense with forest, then bare precipices lifting ghostly snow peaks to an alpine height eighty miles inland. A few days' trek, the explorers thought, would bring them there. But the interior was only accessible up one of the languid, cocoa-brown rivers that twisted through jungle and swamp, adding weeks, months, to a journey. The expedition had picked the Mimika, an unlucky choice.

A base camp was set on the bank of the Mimika near a village, Wakatimi. A thousand Papuans came out to welcome the white men, shouting and dancing, throwing themselves into the river, plastering themselves with mud. Many were so overcome, they shed tears of rapture. The English replied with gifts – empty bottles, sardine tins. It should have been auspicious, but the day after the last load was brought up from the coast the first tragedy struck.

Nobody noticed till after dark that one of the surveyors was missing. Rain fell in torrents, a search of the creeks and pools in the jungle was hopeless. Parties were sent out at dawn, shouting, firing shots in case the young man's bushcraft had saved him; and while Papuans wailed outside his empty tent a grim thought crept up that he may have been murdered, possibly eaten. Eventually his body was found, drowned but intact, and buried under a tree behind the camp: 'The first of the graves of many who left their bones in New Guinea,' Sandy wrote, having read the funeral service to a multicoloured congregation at the edge of the forest. 'Teach us to number our days, that we may apply our hearts to wisdom...'

The arrival of a hundred coolies was no less ominous. At the sight of them a cry went up from Wakatimi that the white men's wives had come to join them – 'and they might well be excused for their mistake,' Sandy noted. In straw hats and bright sarongs, carrying infinite bundles, they didn't look the sort of men, 'to give them a dignity few of them deserved', who might force a track through jungle. The whole sorry lot was paraded on the river bank, youths wretched in physique, crippled by disease, and fifty of the least feeble were picked out, the rest sent back. It was a portent of future troubles. Though replaced several times, batch after batch, the coolies regularly collapsed and mutinied, or fell ill and died.

A party went up the Mimika to set a camp nearer the mountains. The Papuans taken for paddle power and local knowledge kept stopping to eat or sleep, pined for their women, finally stole a canoe and deserted. But after a week's hard going through empty country – the thickest jungle could seem an utter void – they came to a village, Parimau, and another welcome of mud and tears. It was the end of navigable river. Now the task was to bring up the whole expedition and stores before real exploring could begin.

Months passed in desperation, boredom, gloom. Though Wakatimi and Parimau were hardly twenty miles apart it was twice as far by the Mimika, snaking for ever through the jungle, and could take a week, stopping at dusk to pitch tents on a mud bank, liable to be flooded out. When the river rose it was too swift for paddling, too deep for poling, and they toiled upstream by hauling on overhanging branches. When it fell they manhandled the canoes across banks, between rocks, over or under fallen trees; often having to unload the cargo, then tediously reload it.

'The monotony is beyond words,' Sandy wrote in his diary. Breakfast of cocoa and biscuits at dawn, chivvying the coolies for the day's journey, then anything from five to twelve hours sitting on a damp tent with his feet in water sloshing in the canoe. 'The jungle is as ugly as can be – rank undergrowth, scraggy rotting trees. In forty miles I do not think there are half a dozen trees worth looking at.' They grew fast to reach the light, thin and tall, topped with a mass of climbers so heavy it brought the tree down. The jungle floor was strewn with dead wood stinking of decay. Sometimes Sandy took a paddle but got irritated by the coolies working madly for twenty or thirty strokes, then lapsing into 'a haphazard ragtime or doing nothing'. Mostly he watched the muddy banks drift by or took a short cut on foot across a loop of the river.

A solitary flowering creeper, an iguana dozing on a log, snakes curled into the foliage or swimming round the canoes – but little to arouse a naturalist except small bees that swarmed all over him to drink the sweat. And leeches on twigs and leaves, waiting for someone to come brushing past; sucking blood from legs and arms, mouth and eyes, so delicately that they had gorged themselves before being noticed. Butterflies hardly existed, even birds were scarce: a crested pigeon feeding on crabs, a screaming flock of cockatoos to break the great silence, or the cry of a bird of paradise from the forest. 'There is no view to show we are getting near a mountain range... It generally rains hard and you arrive in camp soaking wet... Then see everything taken out of the canoes, tents pitched, food given out... Wet wood is coaxed into boiling a kettle and I get a cup of tea... At six o'clock the meal of the day, rice or a tin... A book and tobacco and to bed about nine or earlier if the mosquitoes are bad.'

At night, through the drumming of rain on the tent, there might be a splash from the river – maybe a crocodile – or the whistle of small reptiles, the lament of a frog-mouth bird, the thunder of a falling tree. Was this the explorer's life Sandy had become a doctor for: slogging up and down a hateful river? Was it any better than the dismal hierarchy of a hospital? He was frustrated, impatient for adventure, or anyway for something pleasanter. 'How I should like to look in on you tonight,' he wrote to his mother in the English spring, 'and hear you play music and smell the good scents coming through the window.' Later, finding common sandpipers migrating to the river: 'What fools to come back to this loathsome country when they might still be up north.' New Guinea was said to be a treasury of natural history, yet he was stuck in 'the most dreary, forbidding country I have seen. There is nothing beautiful in it, nothing of romance, nothing to stir one...' It was the trees, sadly for a man who loved them, that depressed him most: 'Ill-grown and dead, shoving each other out of place, obscuring the view... If I don't get a foot on to that snow I shall consider it a year of my life wasted.'

From Parimau he wrote to a botanist, 'No great discoveries so far, and I fear the chance of making them grows remote... Weather worse every month, coolies sick or dead... It took six months to get ourselves and stuff twenty miles from the coast. The snow is fifty miles further... Never was such a vile country... I would rather be in Africa with fever than in New Guinea without fever.' He even wished himself back 'on one of those interminable roads which I so often cursed.'

But there could be a moment at sunset when the rain cleared, lifting his spirits to a larger view – less stifling, more cosmic. Once it was when Halley's comet trailed its light beam across the sky with Venus moon-like nearby. For several nights it grew enormously, the tail blazing to the zenith till it dwindled and vanished. Sandy couldn't guess its effect on the obscure Papuan mind, but to the coolies it spelt sickness and death.

*

Papuans – a scornful Malay word meaning fuzzy – were as impenetrable as their country, lost in time. To Sandy, cheated of the mountains, this was a chance for another kind of exploration. A naturalist could turn to ethnology, a doctor with cures for sickness could make friends. But too often they reflected the blank, dead-end riddles of the forest. A Papuan's eyes, clear and bright in childhood, quickly turned yellow, blurred – the haunting expression of an animal. If Sandy ever got a man to look him in the eye he looked back into 'an unlighted and empty space'.

They possessed no metal, no pottery. No written vocabulary till Sandy compiled a short dictionary for them. Though they kept a fire burning on a heap of sand in their canoes and a man would carry a smouldering stick into the forest, they had never seen water boiling. Their utensils were coconut shells and bits of bamboo. Their bows were of pandanus wood with a rattan string, decorated with feathers or a crab's claw. Their arrows were reeds tipped with bamboo or a spine from a sting-ray. Their axes were virtually Neolithic, a stone jammed into a hole bored through a shaft of bamboo. At Wakatimi, in wonderment at such anachronism – spying on his own forgotten ancestors – Sandy stood rooted at the sight of a man sharpening axes while a woman wielded another to split a log: 'one of the most primitive scenes I ever witnessed, a glimpse of the Stone Age'.

Carefree, averse to settling anywhere for long, few of them cultivated the soil – a patch of tobacco here and there, or sweet potatoes, bananas – and the search for food was life's business.

From the swamps they fetched wild sago to be kneaded and pulped into grubby lumps, baked in hot embers. When a decayed tree floated down the river it was towed to the bank and chopped up for the maggots in it – a delicacy raw or roasted. But in a land of sudden floods their habit of wandering off to avoid a struggle, and their love of palm liquor, could bring them to starvation. The women would be sent out for wild fruits, lizards and frogs, mussels, crocodile eggs. The men might stir themselves and their dogs to try for a pig, a wallaby or a cassowary in the forest. But they were poor hunters. Sandy watched two men with bows and arrows shooting at an iguana in a tree, missing every time while it climbed slowly out of range. As for the warning of friends at home – that he and his companions would end up cooked for dinner – anyone he questioned showed disgust: 'But that is not proof of their innocence.'

Primitive meant scantily dressed, though as Sandy observed, 'It is a curious thing that a black man never looks naked.' A man might wear a strip of bark from a fig tree or a large shell clipped to the foreskin, 'an ineffectual pretence of decency'. More often he was content with a bamboo penis-case, carved and painted, kept in place by pulling the foreskin through a hole in the end. Women wore bits of bark or grass with a fringe of tassels and shredded leaves, and a bonnet of plaited fibre, pretty enough when new but soon damp and dirty: 'The wearer is a person to be shunned.'

With a shell or bone they cut into their flesh – a cross or circle on the buttocks, a scorpion or crayfish on the arm. They painted their faces red with earth, black with fat and charcoal, white with powdered sago, and pierced their noses to insert the beak of a hornbill or a boar's tusk. In their ears they wore strings of beads, the claw of a cassowary or the Jews' harps brought by the explorers for barter in exchange for stone tools and weapons. But they loved their own music and in times of happiness would hold an all-night concert. Two or three drummers, with cylinders of carved wood, sat by a fire surrounded by the chorus. When a drum's snakeskin slackened after so much beating, it was simply held to the fire till it regained pitch. The chorus hummed, growled, barked, sometimes broke into a rollicking song while the band leader, in a headdress of bird of paradise feathers, tossed and swayed with the music. 'If there is anybody who can becomingly wear those gorgeous plumes', Sandy wrote, 'it is the naked black man.'

Though often exasperated he admired the Papuans' efforts to find a kind of fun in life: their songs and dances, their crude drawings and elaborate cat's cradles, their furious war games with flying spears and brandished clubs. And he had the vision, unusual at the time, to question ideas of settling them in communities: 'Any attempt to "civilize" them must destroy their primitive independence... They do no harm and one dares to hope that such an interesting people may for a long time be left undisturbed.'

*

In a country producing no food every scrap had to be brought in and transported upriver to Parimau. Much of it was eaten on the way, much of it went bad. Tins leaked, sacks of rice were spoilt by rain, dried meat got damp in the climate and had to be re-dried when the sun came out. Some of it, bought cheap in London, was left over from an expedition to the Antarctic. Bully-beef might be fine at the South Pole but here it became pallid lumps swimming in fat, and a cargo of powdered peas would turn the toughest stomach. Faced every evening with another meal from tins they found that if anything induced an appetite better than whisky it was Dutch gin and bitters.

It was nearly a year before enough loads were stacked at Parimau, with enough surviving coolies, to push on into the hills. But life was looking up and Sandy at last felt there was a chance of climbing a mountain. Bearded, close-cropped, leaner than before but fittest among his companions – though unable to shake off the malaria recurring from Africa – he only felt frayed in temper at so much waiting about. Inactivity didn't suit him. But with the diet, the endless delays, the bouts of sickness, it was a harsh test for a dwindling group of individuals. One explorer was dead and two others, racked with fever, had left New Guinea to recuperate. Sandy remained with the last two: 'No doubt we shall rub along together till the end of the expedition,' he told his parents, 'but you can't think how one longs to see fresh people and hear new ideas.'

From his account of their ordeal by flood a bizarre cartoon emerges of three white men in the jungle. The Mimika rose hour by hour, breaking its banks, cutting through the camp. One man, prostrate with fever, lay on a bed raised out of the water on tins while the other two, knee-deep at the table, made a pretence of supper. Any humour to be had was in being able to wash their plates in the river flowing under their chairs, between the first course of biscuits and sardines and the second of biscuits and marmalade: 'An observer looking in on us that evening might well have wondered what kind of lunatics we were.'

Odd moments of drama disturbed the tedium, creeping into Sandy's diary like shafts of sunlight falling briefly in the forest. Two convicts began a quarrel over food and in a flash their knives were out and they were chasing each other through the camp. With a sudden thrust, one stabbed the other in the heart but couldn't escape before he too was dealt a mortal wound. The first died on the spot, the second a few hours later. Another convict, convinced that everyone was against him, spent two days alone in the jungle without food. After Sandy certified him insane, fit only to be sent home, the man was found prowling about with a knife, vowing murder, and was clapped in chains. 'We made friends in a day or two and he was set free, but I confess I was not sorry when we were no longer together.'

At Parimau a fateful truth hit the expedition: they had picked the wrong river; the Mimika would never lead them to the mountains. 'It is fearfully disappointing to have made so little progress,' Sandy wrote. 'So much might have been avoided by finding out the little that was known about this country.' On reconnoitring trips they gazed on jungle stretching infinitely ahead, cut by untold rivers with the peaks as remote as ever. Every morning before the mist came down Sandy would scan the snows, planning routes; perhaps aware of the futility though still hoping. But at least they had quit the noxious lowland. The air was cool and fresh, the water no more the thick soup of lower down, and it was a joy to feel stones underfoot instead of mud.

Eventually the Mimika brought them to a discovery they had never sought. Something in a way more momentous than the first ascent of a mountain. Something unexpected, apocalyptic, to stir a fretting explorer's blood.

*

Two little men were seen one day, and chased like wild animals and caught. Two more were captured while crossing a river. They were midgets beside the Papuans of the low country, but no other race living in the hills was known of. The Papuans called them Tapiro. Sandy called them pygmies and wanted to visit them in their home – an undiscovered people if not an unclimbed mountain. But they were shy, taciturn, and slipped back into the forest.

Sandy wouldn't be put off. From what the Papuans told him it was three miles to the Tapiro village, and he set off with a small party. Three miles of New Guinea jungle, and after ten hours' wandering they had got nowhere. The air was heavy with wild vanilla; they were mocked by the cry of birds of paradise. Though they cut down trees for a compass bearing, they saw only jungle. Puzzled, they could only retreat. Probably the little men were trailing them, watching from the undergrowth.

He tried again with one of the surveyors, taking two Gurkhas to cut a track. After a mile they found a faint path and followed it along fallen trees in a tangle of creepers – 'a fearful struggle to get through'. Then up a valley clogged with trunks, rattans, ferns, to a gorge cutting through a spur of the mountains. Above it, with luck, they would find the Tapiro village. They slithered down to cross a torrent, scrambled up the far side, steep and dense, not knowing which way to go. After six hours it began to rain and the white men were ready to turn back, baffled by so many water courses. But the Gurkhas, confident the village wasn't far, slashed at the jungle with kukris. Did Sandy tell them he had once seen a Gurkha chopping pennies in half? They stumbled over a noose of rattan laid across the path, a pig-trap perhaps, and came out of the forest into a clearing.

Patches of bananas, taro, sweet potatoes. Huts leaning into the hillside. Three little men with bows and arrows standing there in silence. Two more emerged from behind – they had been following through the forest unseen. Others appeared with a bald, white-bearded, one-eyed man disfigured by sores, perhaps the headman. Sandy called out but nobody came forward. No sign of women or children. Timid, perplexed, they seemed neither hostile nor friendly but kept their distance. They refused beads or cloth; they had no use for them or feared a trap. Language was a difficulty. Conversation dried up, the day wore on. That night the explorers got back to camp ten hours after leaving it, drenched, covered with leeches, pleased with their discovery. Luck, or persistence, had thrown up a race of fellow humans new to the white man, as old as the jungle they lived in.

Later the Tapiro came in groups to visit the camp. The Papuan men pounced on the tobacco they brought from the hills, the Papuan women were more interested in the little men themselves and there was an affectionate embrace for one of the visitors, the nearest thing to a kiss in that unlovely place. Emphatically, Sandy noted, they were *little men*: not merely stunted or undersized but 'cleanly built, active-looking little fellows, rather big in the buttocks with well-made calves'. True mountaineers, they walked 'with an easy swinging gait, the knees bent, the body leaning forwards'. They stood bewildered for him to take measurements and reluctantly, after accepting an axe, let him return with them to their village. For an explorer after months of travel with little to show, this was a chance to seize.

Tapiro pygmies

Houses of natives in the mountains

The Tapiro were paler in skin than the Papuans, some of them almost yellow, though so dirty it was hard to tell their true colour. They blacked their faces with grease, lightened their woolly hair with mud. In their sad round eyes Sandy saw something doggy – or dozy – in contrast to their shrill child-like voices. They smiled slowly, they couldn't count beyond two. Over their shoulder they slung a plaited haversack containing tobacco and fire-stick, bits of shell, bamboo, flint for carving and chiselling and sharpening arrowheads – simple, ancient tools. A man might wear a dagger of cassowary bone or a strip of fur in his hair or a helmet of grass and feathers, or a necklace of seeds, claws, wallaby teeth, or a bracelet of twisted rattan, or a boar's tusk in his nose and odds and ends in his ears. But no clothes except one startling item – a unique yellow gourd, a sort of golden codpiece, in which he kept his genitals. Two inches wide at the base, tapering to half an inch at the point and as much as fifteen inches long, it was held erect by a string round the waist: priapism *à la mode* for a Tapiro, a shock of amazement for an Englishman. But modesty went with it and a man who was persuaded to part with his gourd wouldn't remove it in public. He disappeared into the forest and came back with it empty in his hand, a decent covering of leaves in its place.

'Though we never saw the women', Sandy wrote, 'I have no doubt they saw us.' Female voices came out of the jungle, camp fires flickered on the hillside above the village. But the old headman, barking sharply from his hut, kept them out of sight. Perhaps he was afraid that Sandy's Papuans, who were short of women, might steal his own. Even when offered three axes, bringing a glisten to the single eye, he didn't relent.

Over the days Sandy grew fond of the Tapiro, a less improvident people than the Papuans. Their houses, raised on piles and reached by a ladder, were built of split wood and sheets of bark with a palm-leaf roof. In a box of sand a fire was kept burning, with wood hanging above to dry. They reserved a patch of ground by a stream for a latrine, unlike the lazy Papuans. Their arrows were finely carved, their haversacks 'the best attempt at decorative art we saw in the country'. From an instrument of bamboo or bone they extracted faint music – 'pleasing to their ears' but discordant squeaks to Sandy. There was give and take between them. A Tapiro pygmy didn't think much of a box of matches, preferring a loop of rattan and a scrap of dry moss pinched in a cleft stick. With a foot on the stick he sawed the rattan rapidly backwards and forwards under it. In a few seconds the rattan snapped, he picked up the smouldering tinder and blew it into a flame. Sandy managed to light his pipe the Tapiro way 'only with the greatest difficulty'. But he enjoyed their tobacco, bitter but pleasantly strong.

With a touch of envy he wrote of the promising field for some ethnologist living among them. And in the end, as the first white man to disturb their home in the hills with news of another world, he was sad to leave them to a hazy future. Gentle people of the forest, children of nature – and offspring, in a way, of Sandy's own exertion.

*

The expedition had been a year in the country. Stores were running out, coolies and soldiers and convicts were either dead or too sick with fever, dysentery, beri-beri, to carry loads further. Of ten Gurkhas one had died, three had been invalided home. Even the remaining white men became depressed: 'If we were not sick of life we were certainly sick of New Guinea' – and of each other, Sandy implied. Soon it would be time to pack up. But first they would make one last push for the snows. Forlorn perhaps, but at least they might get close enough to find a better route than the Mimika. Sandy was hopeful; he would come back another year with a smaller, stronger party and try a more direct river. 'I spend a good deal of time dreaming plans,' he wrote to his mother. He was provoked by news that a Dutchman had climbed one of the peaks and another expedition was starting. Someone was getting there first. In that strange apocalyptic land it might even be the Duke of the Abruzzi.

With the last of their provisions, enough for twelve days, the three white men and their shrunken band set off – uphill at last: 'There was a peculiar satisfaction in bending one's legs after so long on almost level ground.' Creeping beside a torrent where slices of the hillside had been washed away, climbing past a precipice above a gorge, following a river that thundered over rocks and carried a promise of the heights it came from – it was a change from the monotonous plains. Once or twice they got a glimpse of mountains seeming not so remote. And there was variety in the vegetation: pretty creepers on a bank, a flower-decked tree adding a splash of pink to the eternal green.

Then New Guinea played one of its tricks: a river too swift and deep for wading, blocking further progress. A reward was offered to the first man across and the Gurkhas felled a tree to reach the far side, securing it with a rattan rope. In the night the river rose and swept the tree away, but the rope held and a Gurkha, pulling himself along it hand over hand – caught by the current and dragged horizontal – hung on and won the prize. More ropes were thrown to him and a bridge was built of poles and rattan, a triumph of Gurkha ingenuity transplanted from their Himalayan homeland. But it took precious time; they now had food for only a week.

Higher up they emerged into a world adorned with begonias, arums, nepenthes, aromatic balsams, to delight a botanist. Climbing a mountain spur – climbing against the day when the food ran out – they hoped for a view of unknown country beyond. Two more days, two more camps pitched on ground scratched out of the mountainside. Then over a network of roots and trunks draped with mosses and creepers; clambering over the top branches of the tangle, burrowing through grottoes among the roots. It was a weird, uncanny, variation of Ruwenzori. They came out on a knife-edge ridge; cut down trees to make space for a final camp; put up tents, spread bedding, lit a fire of wild heather, filling the air with incense. For three days it hadn't rained, an aberration in New

Guinea, and there was no water for cooking. But the moss was full of moisture, it was a matter of squeezing it like a sponge. Though the coolies complained of discoloured rice, to Sandy it gave a pleasant, unfamiliar taste. He was always ready to try something new, the local dish or an ad hoc snack – once anyway.

Next day they cut a way up the ridge, hoping for a view, but the clouds came down – another echo of Ruwenzori. The food was nearly finished; they risked one more day and got their reward: precipices rooted in the jungle, lifting peaks to fourteen thousand feet, and far away the phantom snows of the highest, Mount Carstensz. Did Sandy swear a secret promise to himself? I think he did.

Below, the jungle rolled back to the sea forty miles away. Though here and there the sun caught the ribbon of a river there were no features to admire, no colours to gasp at. But there was joy enough: 'Nobody who has not spent a year in a dreary jungle, where you are seldom more than a yard from the nearest tree and the limit of your view is the opposite bank of a stagnant river, can realize the rest – to the eye and to the mind – that a horizon gives.' At last, godlike, he was looking down on a world traversed so painfully.

Then clouds flowed over them; they groped their way down to the camp, to the end of the rice and a chapati of mildewed, weevilly flour. In the following days, retreating by forced marches, stumbling down the track to Parimau and Wakatimi, they mused on the likelihood of being the last as well as the first travellers to penetrate that forsaken land. With no minerals to exploit, no timber worth cutting down, it would be abandoned as it always had been: 'The birds of paradise will call by day, the cassowaries will boom by night, and the leeches will stretch themselves anxiously on their leaves, but it will be a long time before another white man comes to disturb them.'

That man, if Sandy had his wish, would be himself.

*

He couldn't hide his ambivalence. The myth that a tropical forest was where birds of wonderful plumage flashed from tree to tree and brilliant butterflies flitted among exotic blooms, was born in a globetrotter's hothouse. The truth was more drab, and Sandy saw nothing to compare in colour with an English hedgerow: 'You may travel for miles and never see a flower so gaudy as a dandelion.' Half a century later and over a thousand miles east, flogging through jungle in the Solomon Islands on a venture that became a novel, I caught echoes of Sandy's exasperation.

Happily the human mind was selective. A man would forget the rain and mud and leeches, the hunger and nasty food, the unbroken stillness and universal air of death, and remember only the moment when he came out of the twilight and saw the distant mountains. And though in the jungle there might be a thousand things of interest, however blank it seemed, so much time was given to daily needs – the problem of food, the care of the sick, the precautions against flood – that none was left for the hidden wonders round him. A future explorer would live in civilized comfort, taking flying trips into New Guinea's dark heart, finding things still undreamed of: 'But the time for that is not yet, and till then those who plod on foot do the best they can.'

'When I get home,' Sandy told his mother, 'I shall go straight to a place where there are no trees and rejoice in an open view.' He went to Donegal, to fish. In New Guinea, despite his harsh opinion of the coolies, he forgave them for their love of fishing, the hours they spent angling for minnows – 'a sure sign of grace'. In Ireland he was blissfully happy. 'It is almost worthwhile to come for the mutton alone – it is excellent beyond words, not only by reason of the hunger that seasons it.' He was struck too by the beauty of the children, 'in no way connected with the mutton, for their parents tell me they have never eaten meat in their lives. Bare feet, a shawl and no hat is a becoming costume which might well be copied at home...' Perhaps he was thinking of the Tapiro, wearing only a gourd or strands of grass. 'Really, the Irish do appeal to one's sympathy, if not always to one's reason.'

He was asked to write an account of the expedition, and *Pygmies and Papuans* was published in 1912: a solider, more objective work than the Ruwenzori book. The true story, he said, would be 'as wearisome to the reader as it was trying to our patience.' But without giving away his private view of things, he managed to combine real humanity with gentle humour – in elegant classic prose. The explorers who returned had left neither their health nor their bones in New Guinea, unlike many others. They had mapped a vast tract of country, made valuable collections of birds and animals, visited and studied unknown people and brought back stone clubs and axes, feathered headdresses, carved spears, startling penis cases. Yet they had set out with hopes of reaching the Nassau range and it was mortifying to gaze for fifteen months at secret precipices and untrodden snow, to anticipate the final climb to a summit – a dream that kept hopes alive – but in the end to turn back and leave the mountains as mysterious as they had found them, wondering still what might lie on the other side: Sandy's ever real, never reached, Beyond.

*

He wouldn't let go. 'Anyone with a love of mountains,' he said in a lecture to the Alpine Club in London, 'can understand how tantalizing it was, day after day, to see those peaks so close yet unattainable.' And a year after leaving New Guinea he was back, driven by a longing to stand on top and look down on the other side. This time he would take only one white man with him, he would recruit better coolies, he would approach by the Utakwa river, sixty miles further east.

First he went to Borneo to 'catch' Dyaks, the headhunters of the forest – stronger, brighter than Malays who despised them. Travelling deep into the country, delighting in a gibbon swinging through the trees, criss-crossing the equator sixteen times in three days, tramping between one waterlogged village and the next: he liked the Dyaks straightaway – 'jolly fellows, strong enough for anything' – and after he had cured several of cholera they seemed pleased with him too. At a place where the day's heat was flavoured with the stink of a dead crocodile in the river he took a sampan for a solo evening cruise: 'They are rather astonished at my knowing how to do it, and think me a fool to paddle myself.' When a man asked him where he was going and Sandy waved a hand vaguely over the river, the man said, 'Ah, Master goes to eat the wind.' These wild men were poets too.

Some of the Dyaks

His affection for them was clinched one night after paddling upriver to a crowded house lit by torches. He was given a chair in the middle, drinks were pressed on him, tasting like stale ginger beer, and a chorus of women sang in his honour: how glad they were to see him, how they hoped he would stay and be their raja, how they all wanted to go with him to New Guinea, how Master Allah must be something like him. A narrow plank was laid on the ground for dancing – solo male performances, leaps and poses of vivid beauty to the music of drums and oboes. Out of the dark into the torchlight a man would spring from end to end of the plank in bird-like bounds, or step delicately along it in a sequence of curving limbs and body – comic, lithe, suggestive: 'Every man was almost perfectly made.' Later, in feathered hats and monkey-fur cloaks, they mimed fighting, killing an enemy, cutting off his head. Sandy found it hard to reconcile such urbanity with their notorious ferocity. Human heads hung in bunches from the roof, 'and they are always ready to add to the collection.' But it was a long time since they had taken a white man's so he had no fear for his own.

Would the Dyaks happily leave their swampy land and travel two thousand miles across the sea? First they must sleep on it, and if they had good dreams they would come with him. Next day they agreed and with a month's pay, 'a monstrous sum for people of this kind', they went to a Chinese store to buy soap and perfume for the voyage, emerging in ridiculous clothes: men who had never worn a coat or trousers grinning with pride, being chaffed by their friends, looking 'perfectly frightful'. They were lodged in prison, out of harm while waiting for a ship, and threatened to make trouble at sea – dangerously volatile passengers straight from the forest among solid Dutch colonials. But they were excited by everything on board and the steam whistle, every time it went off, was greeted with echoing hoots of laughter. They were children, full of fun though never losing touch with a heritage of savagery.

A base camp was set on the Utakwa river. Sandy had hired Kloss, a museum curator, as zoological and botanical collector, and with seventy Dyaks and an escort of soldiers and convicts under a Dutch sergeant there were two hundred and twenty men – 'far too many and damned too much baggage'. Seventeen tons of rice, a ton of dried pork, half a ton of dried fish with quantities of tea and sugar as well as tents, blankets, clothes for each man and balaclavas and moccasins for those likely to climb high, and twelve shotguns with ammunition: it was a daunting pile on the river bank. But at sunset Sandy was cheered by a glimpse of the snows of Mount Carstensz, the glory of the Nassau range, calling him on. And after dark a tree alight with fireflies, a vision of magic from a fairytale, seemed a good omen.

The Dyaks scorning Sandy's tents, he gave them two days to build their own wood-and-pandanus houses, then had them cutting down trees for canoes: hollowing out the trunk, opening it further with hooks and weights over a fire, adding thwarts, carving a monster figurehead. They worked keenly though often knocking off for a smoke or a bathe, or to chase a turtle with spears and paddles, swimming underwater, breaking the surface with a blowing, spluttering face; and on moonlit nights they held dancing, jumping, wrestling contests, shouting with laughter when a man fell. Sandy never tired of watching them: 'I like them immensely and I think they like me, which is all to the good.'

His plan was to go up the Utakwa as far as possible by canoe, make a food depot and cut a way in three-day stages through the foothills. The weather was fine, the men were healthy and enjoying themselves – it was a different New Guinea from last time. And instead of floods the river was low; they had to chop a passage among fallen trees, haul the canoes over rocks and shallows. But there were no welcoming villages along the river, just an occasional shelter for wandering Papuans in search of breadfruit. At first the Dyaks had only contempt for them, then were struck by the idea of Papuan heads hanging up at home in Borneo – fresh, rare, the envy of the neighbours.

They got a chance when some knives were stolen. Fired with greed, armed for the hunt, they piled into a canoe to give chase. Sandy saw what would happen: natives killed by the white man's coolies, his reputation for friendliness destroyed, other natives too frightened to visit his camp; and he ordered the Dyaks out of the canoe. Shouting, cursing, they turned their rage on him. Somehow he soothed them and said he would go with them. Mercurial, impulsive, instantly happy again: thirty Dyaks hungering for murder, paddling hell-bent down the river, crammed into a canoe with an English explorer and a Dutch sergeant with a rifle. But the Papuans had a long start and got away; and the Dyaks, cheated of trophies, asked Sandy's permission to cut off the heads of any more they met.

Inevitably the expedition was waylaid by mishaps. An unexpected flood carried away the canoes, and though some were brought back they were badly smashed: 'It is really confounded bad luck.' One of the convicts, swimming across the river, sank in the middle. Sandy sent out Dyaks in a canoe to save him but he was never found, only a row of bubbles drifting downstream. Two days later, trying to get up the Utakwa to the depot, a canoe struck an underwater snag and capsized. Though most of the baggage was recovered a lot of food went to the bottom – 'a fearful loss' and a portent of a worse shipwreck to come. Then a Papuan who had stolen a pickaxe was shot dead by the escort – 'a dreadful piece of news' which would reach into the mountains, to the unknown people Sandy hoped to meet. Instead of making friends he would be shunned, a gun-toting intruder to beware of.

Six weeks after entering the Utakwa – fifty miles from its mouth, another fifty to the snows – Sandy struck out from the river into the jungle with Kloss and the Dutch sergeant and a party of Dyaks; cutting a way towards the foothills, slogging for a week over forest-drenched ridges and intervening streams. There were signs of human life – patches of tobacco, ginger, bananas, bits of chewed sugarcane and bones, even two penis gourds – but any natives kept out of sight.

'Struggled on through very bad ground... Along a high steep ridge... Up a hill and got a glorious view of the mountains – lights and shadows not to be described... If we can reach the foot of the snow we can reach the top... Down to a stream, the first we have touched for two days, where the Dyaks killed a poisonous snake and skinned it for the meat... They are the jolliest people I have ever travelled with... A heavy thunderstorm ending in a hurricane... There is such a lot to do and these next four months are too short... If we can look over to the other side and see further ranges beyond – perhaps higher, no man knows – it will be worth all the grief and pain... Everything depends on the Dyaks... They are splendid fellows – I begin to have quite an affection for them... If they stand the cool climate and the unaccustomed rocks we shall have a fair chance of success... Have begun to make a map of the mountains and have taken telephotos – not absolute failures...'

Though pursued by setbacks Sandy held the expedition together, while fending off his malaria and in pain from a wrenched foot. Did he ever show the unpleasant side of his character that Charles Rothschild had suspected? Perhaps it didn't exist; there is nobody now to ask. A tin of beef and rice and a plum pudding for Christmas dinner, sitting under a leaky fly-sheet with guttering candles and streams of water underfoot, was an attempt at seasonal cheer. And on New Year's Eve: 'Dog tired, but drank a bottle of Rothschild's champagne and blessed him.'

Further into the hills they were guided by natives to a river where men from the mountains, with women and children and pigs, stopped them going further. After much palaver an old man poured a gourd of water into the river, threw a stone after it, shouted a secret spell and led the party up the river, wading through gorges between rock walls, finally vanishing up a waterfall too steep for Sandy's men to follow. But at least they had made contact with the mountain natives – friendly and fearless, not small enough to be pygmies. They painted their faces red or black, they wore a boar's tusk in the nose and necklaces of teeth, rats' bones, bits of shell; and carried bows and arrows, stone axes and knives, sometimes a spoon made from the shoulder blade of a pig for scooping out a sweet pota-to. A man's dress was the familiar yellow gourd but with a knotted tassel hanging over it like a sporran; they had an odd habit of clicking the gourd to show surprise. A woman's brief petticoat of bark cloth seemed always to be slipping off behind.

For weeks they led Sandy along hunting tracks; up and down steep ridges, across rivers, towards the mountains. Once they came to a clearing in the forest where a 'savoury-smelling' feast of potatoes, yams, chunks of pork, was being cooked over hot stones. People pointed mysteriously to a fine new house, raising the right nostril with the right thumb – a sign of disgust. Inside a man sat by the fire, decrepit, diseased, covered in sores but not apparently near death. He was glad to smoke Sandy's tobacco, and Sandy felt something was expected of him but couldn't tell what. When he returned later the house had been burnt to the ground with the remains of human bones among the ashes. Had the man died and been cremated? Had his family, unwilling to feed him any longer, prepared a funeral feast before knocking him on the head and setting fire to the house? They had all disappeared, there was no way of finding out.

Trekking from camp to camp, visited by natives, Sandy learnt to return their greeting – a trick of brow-raising, head-nodding, constant smiling. But it was frustrating to understand hardly a word among people so fond of talking, crowding round his tent to the point of over-intimacy: 'They pull me about, stroke me, tug my hair and beard, poke inside my clothes, and generally fondle me in a way I am quite unused to.' Though he was amenable to local habits, a cuddle was going too far. He was uneasy too among a crowd who set up a weird barking noise, dancing, prancing, waving bows and arrows, then swooping on Sandy's party with a peculiar gesture of friendship – interlocking knuckles, snatching them apart with a loud 'Wah!' repeated many times. The leader ordered silence, launched into a speech and presented Sandy with a white pig; and the ceremony ended with the people agreeing to guide him through their country to the mountains.

*

They camped beside a bubbling mountain stream; and by a hot sulphur spring where violets and begonias grew; and in uplands where thick forest gave way to pines and casuarinas, where Sandy found orchids, meadowsweet, rhododendrons, a geranium, a blue gentian. It was getting hopeful. Mount Carstensz appeared less then ten miles ahead. But the ground got steeper, the party had to be roped with lengths of rattan: 'The weight of men made the vegetation start to slide down the smooth rock, and not much more would have set the whole thing avalanching... No footholes at all... We had to make a bridge with a sapling thrown from boulder to boulder, bending like a fishing-rod... No crack or projection to give a handhold... A slip would mean being swept into the torrent like a piece of grass... I was glad when we were past... Camped in a mossy jungle and slept snug enough...'

Without the natives they would never have got through such country, but two days later, camped in clouds on a high ridge, even the guides were lost. Next morning, before the daily rainstorm, the world cleared for a view back to the country they had been through, and down the Utakwa valley to the flat jungle stretching to the sea. They scrambled over scree to a rock wall where a native found a way up – 'they can climb like squirrels' – and lowered a rope for the others. Then on to the first patch of snow with a glacier hanging above. Carstensz towering overhead was nearly conquered, but it was midday, too late to go further.

Next day, with Kloss and a few Dyaks, Sandy set off to put a camp as high as possible for the last assault. It was raining and blowing and half the Dyaks, miserable with cold, dropped their loads and turned tail. The rest struggled through dense mist to camp on steep, lumpy ground with everything soaking. 'There we spent a night which, even by the low standard of New Guinea comfort, was the most disagreeable I can remember... But we had an exceedingly fine dinner off a tin of mutton which had always been sloppy tasteless stuff – now it was hard and firm and excellently tasty. Also half a tin of plum pudding with a dash of brandy from my flask, and then all our water in cocoa, which gave us a small cupful each. It was all very good had we not been so tremendously hungry... The Dyaks kept a fire going in their tent, but nobody got much sleep.'

In the morning Sandy and Kloss climbed through fog and rain to the foot of the snow, then up a glacier to a point between a wall of rock and a wall of ice. Three strong climbers could have gone on, but Kloss had never been on a mountain and in such weather 'it was not to be thought of... Nothing for it but to turn back.' Boiling the hypsometer gave a height of nearly 15,000 feet, leaving perhaps an hour's climb to the ridge between the two peaks of Carstensz. 'To have the prize withheld when it was within our grasp was almost more than Christian patience could bear... If we had gone a few hundred feet higher, what might we have seen beyond? Further and further ridges?' The answer would be found 'by the happy person who first reaches the watershed and looks over to the other side'. Crushed, mortified, they stumbled back to the camp: 'Our food was at an end, the men wretched with cold. Fires won't burn properly because of damp wood, rice won't cook properly because of the low boiling-point. Stomachs are out of order as well as spirits.' In the following days, on the long retreat down the Utakwa valley, Sandy's disappointment was mitigated a little by looking back and seeing Carstensz always in cloud. Nobody up there would have had a view.

It was a retreat from blighted hopes but not from troubles. A week after leaving the top camp, returning through the forest, they came on a dead man, and a little later a dead woman. Then another man, two women, a child, a third man. Over the next days they found forty bodies, some in rough shelters, others tied with pandanus leaves and buried in shallow holes, mostly lying on the track where they had died. In a leaf hut there was a little girl alive with a man and woman and another child dead beside her. Kloss carried her all day and tried to feed her, but she died in the night. There was no sign of disease; it was a mystery explained only by improvidence and starvation. These people had come down from the mountains

The last trees, 10,500ft

View from 14,000ft

to visit the white man's camp. Their sweet potatoes had run out, they had begged from the coolies who had nothing to spare, they had eaten raw palm-hearts and roots before starting on the journey home: up and down for days on end through foodless jungle, growing weaker, hampered by families and pigs. Such human devastation would haunt Sandy for ever: a picture of a hopeless, heartbreaking country where the inhabitants, ekeing a hand-to-mouth existence, couldn't keep themselves alive: 'They just give up and die, as natives can.'

A more personal tragedy struck after they had reached the depot on the Utakwa. 'Resting our weary bodies, filling our empty bellies, sleeping, reading newspapers... Am also improving my map... Quite a pleasant time.' After sending men and stores downriver, Sandy followed in a canoe with six Dyaks. The water was high after a night of rain, they hit a snag in the worst of the rapids, the canoe turned over. Sandy and a Dyak scrambled on to it and went careering downstream to a big tree lying out from the bank, partially underwater. The Dyak jumped off the canoe but Sandy, weighted by clothes and boots, was caught among submerged branches and pulled down into the dark where 'things looked very black'. With a frantic struggle he got free and came up half dead; then was carried by the current 'at a hideous pace, now and again touching the ground with my feet, but utterly helpless'. Half lying, half crouching, he was swept towards more rapids 'which would certainly have ended my troubles'. But the Dyaks grabbed him and hauled him to the bank 'where I felt pretty bad for some time.'

The canoe was salvaged but the sack with Sandy's belongings – diary, map and plane table, camera and lenses and many instruments, medicine chest, bedding, folding table and chair, silver brandy flask and much else – was lost. 'Desperate and hopeless condition. Within an ace of being drowned into the bargain, so I ought not to complain, but it is hard to be philosophic.'

*

Sandy's Utakwa expedition was over. 'I shall be very sorry to say goodbye to my Dyaks… They are nearly all fit but pretty fagged out.' He had lost three men – one by drowning, one by dysentery, one by fever – a better record than the Mimika expedition when twenty men had died. He had collected flora and fauna, had mapped unknown country, had been the first to tread the snows of the Nassau mountains. But though he failed to climb a peak his two explorations of New Guinea were the most original and distinguished of his career; and the Royal Geographical Society presented him with the Gill Memorial Prize and later the Patron's Gold Medal.

In London he gave a lecture to the Society. Afterwards a veteran explorer stood up and told the audience how hard it was, sitting comfortably in Kensington after dinner, to grasp the appalling truth of the journey, an epic told by a man in evening dress looking as if he had never been out of Piccadilly. Then a Dutch explorer who had been in New Guinea commended Sandy on his kind-heartedness to the natives: 'When Dr Wollaston got into difficulties he had their help – that is how an Englishman gets on.' And the president, calling for a vote of thanks, said he had never listened to a more striking lecture. It was a special pleasure to hear a man who not only had the gift of friendship with strange peoples but whose spirit of adventure was far from exhausted – he had been stopped by a mere ice wall from climbing Carstensz and was unlikely to be put off from trying again.

Years later, after the Great War, Sandy listened with mounting irritation to a lecture at the Society by an Australian official, entitled *The Opening of New Territories in Papua*. At the end he offered some remarks which he was confident the audience would disagree with. 'It is nice to see the world opened up,' he said. 'We like to see new railways on our maps and Africa dotted with aerodromes and such things. But I don't think we sufficiently consider the point of view of the people whose countries are opened up... The lecturer objects to inter-tribal warfare. Well, we have just spent years killing each other to make the world free for democracy. Now and again the Papuans kill one or two people to celebrate a festival, or because the country doesn't produce mutton... I don't think it is quite fair to inflict what we are pleased to call our western civilization on these people. You call them savages. Many of them – not those you have seen photos of tonight but their cousins a few hundred miles to the west – are friends of mine. I have always found them to be happy and cheerful, sufficiently fed and suitably clad. So far as I know they are as truthful as most of us... The lecturer says we must alter, or modify, their traditions – "institutions", I think, is the word – so that they "fall into line with the needs of progress". I hope they will go slowly about this modifying of institutions... You have in New Guinea the last people, I believe, who have not yet been contaminated, if that isn't an unkind word, by association with the white races. They have an extraordinarily interesting culture of which we know very little, and we have much to learn from them... I suppose it is too much to expect the whole of the interior of New Guinea to be kept as a vast ethnological museum, but I should like to believe that a really large area – there is plenty of room – is kept as a reserve where these people can live their own life and work out their own destiny, whatever it may be. And into that country no traders, no missionaries, no exploiters, not even police, should be allowed to go... Perhaps it is an impossible dream, but I am looking ahead through two or three centuries, and the fate of the Tasmanians and the present condition of the aboriginal Australians might be sufficient warning.'

He had a vision, as so often, of a shimmering, not impossible Beyond.

*

Never having known Sandy, though he was my father, I came to rely for a picture on quotations and the memory of people who had met him or been his friend. Otherwise, apart from a few incidents in my very early life, fragile but precious, I kept only a sense of his presence: a person Mary talked to, less substantial than his clothes, pipe, tobacco tins. For years, greedy for whatever I could get hold of, I would treat anyone who added to the portrait as a messenger bringing fresh news. 'I remember him,' somebody wrote, 'as a quiet, reserved man with an amused smile at the general scene,' and I got another glimpse. But as his generation vanished into the past, the hope of a first-hand report became remote.

Fifty years after his death, at a party in the London zoo – one of Sandy's boltholes as a medical student – I met an old Cambridge professor: a mountaineer, literary pundit, poet. When we were introduced and through the party noise, through the cries from monkey cage and parrot house, the professor heard my name he asked if I was the explorer's son. It was a chance to pick the memory of one of Sandy's friends and he told me something I hadn't heard before. Something mythic and illuminating which he had got from Sandy and gave a view of him in a strange light.

It concerned that second expedition to the mountains of New Guinea: part of Sandy's story – I knew it well. But here was someone who had heard it straight from Sandy. Not a geographer but a poet whose vision of exploring was romantic, with naked savages, poisoned arrows, a whiff of cannibalism. And to the account of the retreat to the coast – over endless ridges of the foothills, along tortuous jungle tracks, down infested streams that backed and turned for ever – the professor supplied a twist. The party was struck by fatigue and sickness and the terrible climate and Sandy, himself weak with malaria, struggled to bring them out alive. But mercifully, through tropical mists, heat haze, rainstorms, he was led on by another white man far ahead – the back view of a stranger travelling in the same direction towards the coast. Each time Sandy topped another ridge, the man was going over the further one. Each time Sandy turned another bend of a path or river, the man was disappearing round the next.

Yet was he really a stranger? He looked maddeningly familiar and even in his feverish state – even at such a distance – Sandy thought he recognized him from somewhere in the past, but could never catch up to make sure. When he got close enough to shout, the man wouldn't stop or turn to show his face. Could he be the same Englishman who had thrown away his breeches high on Ruwenzori? All Sandy knew was that another explorer, pressing on in front, kept him going and rescued the expedition.

At last they reached the coast where the stranger gave him the slip once more and disappeared for good. Though Sandy tried to solve the riddle, making enquiries about other travellers in the country, he discovered nothing. He paid off his coolies and on the long voyage home forgot about it, till months later in London he went to be measured for a suit. In the fitting-room he tried on the jacket and watched the tailor marking the front, snipping, pinning, then turning him round to show him the back. There in the mirror was the mystery man Sandy had followed in the jungle, the *doppelgänger* who had saved his life.

The story was told me by a man for whom sensitivity to poetry, creating something truer than the facts, was testimony to a life of imagination. And it gave a new dimension – rich, literary, tantalizing – to my father's image. Another phantom to pursue.

IV THE GREAT WAR

'I shall probably come straight back to England to look for another chance of getting away from it,' Sandy had written from New Guinea.

Between expeditions there were long gaps – recovering from the last, preparing for another. But Sandy had no money, he scraped and scoured, a bachelor without ties living on next to nothing. Briefly he was public health officer at Guildford, a penance that must have jarred with dreams of travelling beyond Surrey. He wrote articles, gave lectures, and for a time was natural history editor of *Country Life*: 'A man of remarkable parts', they said fulsomely. 'His manner of doing his work was as pleasant as its matter was excellent.' He escaped to go fishing, not in the smart English chalk streams but in the cheaper, wilder waters of Sutherland or Donegal. He was asked to write the life of his old zoology professor, an early champion of Darwin, and said he couldn't keep afloat on less than a hundred pounds 'for paper and candles' while he worked. He went often to Cambridge, reserving a place in his heart for King's College. And in London, from his lodgings in a humbler part of town, he would go to the Savile Club in Piccadilly for dinner in congenial like-minded company.

In other all-male clubs the members tended to share the same profession or politics. The Savile drew men – bishops and atheists, millionaires and near-paupers, writers and artists but scientists too – without heed for class, religion, race, but for their conviviality or some rare contribution to the talk. Once when a candidate was proposed for the club a member muttered nervously, 'I think he's probably been a Borstal boy,' to which another replied, 'That should make him more interesting.' In the dining-room they sat at a long communal table instead of separate small tables – less stuffy, more stimulating. It cost two guineas a year to belong, dinner was three shillings.

It was at the Savile, the day before war broke out in August 1914, that Sandy's life for the next five years was settled. The place buzzed with scares and rumours, and across the table another member launched into a harangue about the army's urgent need for doctors. Though medicine was far from uppermost in Sandy's life, merely a way to pursue the calling of naturalist and explorer, he was annoyed by the man's presumption and suggested the navy might want doctors too, probably before the army began to stir. But the man wouldn't listen and was such a bore that Sandy made up his mind to throw in his lot with the navy. Next morning he went to the Admiralty. He was thirty-nine and was told that at forty he would be too old. He was given a medical exam, feeling an idiot climbing a rope and hopping round the room naked, and by the second day of the war he was a Temporary Surgeon R.N. Though he had avoided the army it was a nuisance – he had planned a fort-night's fishing with a friend in Scotland.

Two days later a telegram came ordering him 'forthwith' to join the *Mantua* at Tilbury docks. He packed up, wrote letters all night, caught a train at dawn and reached Tilbury for breakfast. Remembering the navy was either clean-shaven or bearded he clipped off his moustache in the train. But 'forthwith' wasn't as urgent as it sounded. The *Mantua* was a luxury P&O liner being converted into an armed merchant cruiser. Guns had to be fitted, decks strengthened, everything painted grey – noisy, dirty days with workmen camping in the cabins and saloons. When unnecessary woodwork was removed, Sandy's love of good carpentry was wrenched at the sight of fine panels and fittings, pride of a famous passenger line, being hacked out and piled on the dockside. But nobody knew the ship's destiny – possibly patrolling trade routes in the Mediterranean or down to South America. Most people believed Germany would collapse and the war would be over in a few months, but Sandy was sceptical: 'Thirty years is doubtless too long a guess, but I don't think it so wide of the mark as Christmas is... Heaven send I am wrong.'

He got into uniform, 'eight flaming brass buttons and two bands of gold braid with a strip of red – for blood presumably... The peaked cap is an abominable thing'. But it only reminded him that he was wasting glorious summer weather when he should be on a Scottish loch. Eventually, with coal bunkers full and the prospect of a long voyage before another sight of land, the *Mantua* slipped out of the docks, downriver and into the English Channel. Then it was rumoured that they were heading north through the Irish Sea to Orkney. So much for Sandy's tropical white ducks.

Most of the seamen were North Sea fishermen: 'As fine a lot as you would see anywhere,' Sandy wrote, but the stokers were 'of the less desirable class of Eastender with a dash of Liverpool Irish'. There was also a squad of marines on board, 'good steady fellows' except the bugler who liked to blast off behind one's back – a joke that Sandy stopped by putting him

A.F.R. Wollaston, 1914

on the sick list. They all had to be drilled into the naval way of things, and off Ireland trial shots were fired from each gun, shuddering through the thin, unwarlike hull. 'We could put up a fair show against any smaller ship, but heaven help the *Mantua* if we run into anybody with a six-inch gun. We are an enormous target, bigger than any battleship, and should go to the bottom like a stone.' As doctor to a healthy crew leading a healthy life Sandy found time on his hands, which he never liked, and began compiling *Letters of a Naval Surgeon* as a diversion.

Anchored at Scapa Flow in Orkney, they were inspected by an admiral and given their orders: to patrol the sea between Shetland and Norway, back and forth, and stop and search every ship they met. 'So we have been given a very honourable post at the mouth of the North Sea, on a line that will be taken by any German that gets out.' On their first trip they picked up a wireless report of submarines and heard gunfire, but the air waves were intercepted and they could only steam on to Norway and back. And there again and back, for months on end.

Soon the *Mantua*'s beat was extended to the Hebrides, the Faroes, Iceland – cruising up and down at ten knots night and day, challenging everything that sailed or steamed and, if no satisfactory reply, sending across a boat with an officer and boarding party. In bad weather it was a fine test of seamanship. Lowering the boat from davits high above the water, catching the moment to cast off as a wave surged up – bad timing could upset the boat and drown the crew; then a heavy pull through the overwhelming sea to the other ship which lay lifting and dropping, often failing to make a lee for the boat; waiting alongside while the officer took his chance, jumped at the swinging ladder, climbed up the ship's side to check the papers; finally the whole trip in reverse till the boat was hoisted safely aboard the *Mantua*. If the papers weren't in order the ship was sent to the nearest British port, with an officer and marines who were glad of a break in the monotony.

A steamer from Iceland to Denmark carried a cargo of ponies 'presumably for the sausage machine'. It was rough weather, the pens in the hold had been smashed and at every roll two hundred ponies slid from side to side in a kicking squealing mass. Sandy thought of Conrad's account in *Typhoon* of Chinese coolies being transported. And on a Danish mailboat there was an Englishwoman who was scared of minefields and asked to be taken on board the *Mantua*. It was weeks before she was put ashore, and Sandy smiled to see the officers hanging about the only skirt in sight, 'a strapping athletic girl – hospital nurse type'. He was more interested in glaucous gulls, smews, great skuas flying off the cliffs of Shetland, and a view of the mountains of Skye close enough to pick out the pinnacles he had climbed: 'What good times I have had up there!'

Then down to Liverpool for coaling. He went ashore for

dinner and a music-hall: 'beastly place – all very depressing'. And back to the North Sea patrol. Rumours seemed more valid than the rare bits of news, and off Norway it was whispered that the *Mantua* was a decoy to lure enemy warships out of the fiords, 'an unpleasant role as we have neither speed nor guns worth anything'. Alarm bells rang, everyone rushed to action stations, eyes were skinned for periscopes: 'Something is going on but we don't know what... Not very great sport for us.'

The first of the winter gales was on them, there would soon be only a few hours of daylight. 'We are hoping we shall not be kept north all winter,' Sandy told his mother. 'I should greatly prefer to go into the tropics or thereabouts... My shipmates are a very decent lot and we get on all right, but I sometimes wish for some more understanding persons to talk to... We are all more or less bearded and we shall be grey before this is over.' But instead of the tropics the *Mantua* was sent on a secret mission to Arkhangel in north Russia. Too big to reach the port they were met at the mouth of the Dvina river by a steamer with a cargo of gold bars, guarded by soldiers in beards and furs. The Russian officers bemoaned their liquor rationing and made the most of the *Mantua*'s visit. For Sandy the days at anchor in the estuary were a treat. Cloudless arctic weather 'cold enough for a tropical animal', with nights aglow with aurora borealis, aloud with flights of wild geese and duck: 'A time that made one glad to be alive, fit to walk across the world instead of being cooped up in a floating box.'

On the voyage back, after a warning signal, the unwieldy *Mantua* zigzagged down the Irish Sea to dodge torpedoes. But in Liverpool they learnt that the danger was from mines and by zigzagging they had doubled the chances of being sunk. It showed up the haphazard conduct of naval warfare. And the view through drizzle of a blank dock wall, though a change from the everlasting sea, was only a reminder of the impotence of Sandy's present life. Terrible battles were being fought in France; he felt ashamed of his inaction. He had volunteered for this, he wasn't being properly occupied, he should be planning a third expedition to New Guinea. The snows of Carstensz hovered on a horizon far beyond these northern seas. 'This is a desperately stagnating existence,' he told a Cambridge friend. 'I would rather be alone with Dyaks in New Guinea than with three hundred and fifty white men on board ship.' And King's College, like a willing but unreachable mistress, loomed ever on the fringe of consciousness: 'I had a terrible dream of bombs being dropped on Cambridge – most vivid. I was high up in, I think, Gibbs' building.'

A more pressing nightmare was the present season of storms: 'They are not waves but moving mountains,' he wrote, half wishing them to be rock and ice, wondering how the *Mantua* could climb the next. At the top of each ridge the sea was picked up by the wind – 'but wind is not the word for the force that lives in these latitudes' – and hurled at the ship. Built to carry thousands of tons of cargo, now in ballast and high in the water, the liner rolled and pitched dramatically: 'I have seen the Atlantic at its most terrible and was often horribly afraid. But I have got to the stage of losing fear, if one really can…' It was no comfort to hear that two similar merchant cruisers had gone down with all hands, not holed by the enemy but swamped by the sea. After the loss of one of them, the *Mantua* went to search the waters where it was last heard of. In broad daylight, less than half a mile away, Sandy saw a boat full of men – distinct for a few seconds. A big sea was running, the *Mantua* was rolling heavily, the boat vanished. Sandy raced up to the bridge but nobody else had seen anything; the vision had gone. Was it a hallucination? He wasn't a psychic man, but the phantom boat was as acutely real as the explorer who had led him out of the New Guinea jungle. For the rest of his life he was troubled by the thought of shipwrecked sailors being left to drown.

*

Censoring the crew's letters was the doctor's job and Sandy found it poignant, often amusing: 'I am greatly struck by the number of letters to what the lower deck calls its "best girl"… I begin to think I have missed a lot by not having had a best girl. I wish I could go back twenty years.'

Christmas, during a lull between gales, was celebrated in naval fashion. After church in the saloon with a psalm for those who go down to the sea in ships and lusty cries for those in peril on the sea, ending with Nelson's last prayer, the captain led his officers and a party of clowns in fancy dress, with drums and trumpets and whistles, on a tour of the ship. They stopped at each mess – decorated to look like home with paper flowers, garlands, messages of peace and goodwill – for a taste of plum duff and a speech by the captain. 'Wonderful people, these sailors!' Sandy said, and in a singsong afterwards it stirred his egalitarian heart to see officers and stokers, as drunk as each other, swinging hand in hand, bawling out *Auld Lang Syne*; lost in sentimentality, forgetting the trials they had been through – Englishmen together at war.

On Christmas night they were hit by the worst storm imaginable. For three days they were hove-to, heading into the wind with only speed for steerage way. By the time the weather eased they had drifted far off course and had to turn – a dangerous manoeuvre in such a sea. Caught with the wind beating against the ship's length, holding the balance between bow and stern, it needed power to break out of the vice; but too much power, if the propellers were lifted out of the water, meant the engines racing to destruction. 'My most miserable moments have been when the ship turns broadside on to the sea. As she goes over you instinctively hold on to something – though what good that does I don't know – and for one horrible moment she pauses and swings back... It is all so wearisome and one's body cries out for rest.' It was impossible to intercept another ship going through the same ordeal; impossible even to fix their own position.

War, like exploring, could be wastes of tedium broken by moments of significance: enduring one, keeping alert for the other. But for Sandy, even in twenty-two days without sight of land, it was a chance to get acquainted with the headlong-plunging gannet and, even better, the astonishing fulmar gliding, banking over the waves, tirelessly following the ship in the heaviest weather: 'I should like to know more about the life of the fulmar.' Sometimes they passed a famous bird place – the island home of the last great auk, the lonely cliff where the sea eagle once nested – or there was a glimpse of the Sutherland mountains, the magnificent St Kilda cliffs, the Faroes deep in snow and said to be a refuge for German submarines: 'We pretend not to bother about them, but they do get on people's nerves.' There might be an alarm and a rush to action stations, and blind shots fired at what looked like a conning tower before returning to the long slog: ploughing up and down an empty sea with only a whale or school of porpoises to look at.

Every few weeks they went to Liverpool or Glasgow for coaling, and early in 1915 Sandy had forty-eight hours' leave at a highland hotel: 'Most beautiful in winter with nobody here.' But he felt uneasy ashore: 'One has no right to be loafing about when the army is up to the neck in mud.' Many of his friends were in the Flanders trenches or already dead: 'Awful slaughterings – how many of us will be left at the end?' At least in a ship he had a dry bed and plentiful, regular food. It was nothing like the discomfort of New Guinea where, but for the war, he would soon be starting on his third expedition. Now it looked a forlorn hope: 'We shall not be beaten, that is certain. But can we win?' On board the *Mantua* only the captain, who often invited the ship's doctor to his cabin on the bridge, shared his belief that they were in for a long haul. Overcome by a strange fatalism Sandy wrote to the Cambridge friend, 'I wish I could come and have a look at you,' as though he never expected another chance. Previously on some desperate venture – 'and I never told you the half of the risks in New Guinea' – he had always felt sure of coming back. But this time he vaguely doubted if they would dine together in King's again: 'Very likely I am wrong, but I have a curious instinct in these things.'

To a rare woman friend, the one he would one day marry, he wrote: 'It is a most glorious spring day and I just tingle with a longing to be on land and to smell the good earth. I cannot think why the Almighty made this huge desert of water. It seems such an awful waste of time to be ploughing up and down at sea, and I grudge every moment of it... I should like to go to sleep for a few years and wake up when it is over... I wish I could believe in reincarnation or in any other comfortable belief... There is plenty of time for reading at sea, but it is difficult to concentrate in a wallowing ship, and I have done nothing solid these eight mortal months... I am sorry to inflict all this grumbling stuff on you, but much solitude at sea is bad for one's manners.'

Often they challenged fishing-boats: 'Wonderful little craft – they ride over the huge seas as lightly as seagulls.' It was said that some had been captured by the Germans and sent back to sea with mines to be laid in British waters. On one of the roughest days when the *Mantua* was plunging about, pouring water from end to end, they passed a Yarmouth trawler lying hove-to, her decks dry, the crew sitting smoking in the lee of the deckhouse. Another day they hailed a brigantine under full sail, homeward bound from Iceland to Bideford. To Sandy it was a joy to hear West Country voices over the water. Later he felt another stab of nostalgia and blessed the *Mantua*'s designers for it: she had been built for hot climates, letting in as much air as possible – no pleasure in the North Atlantic winter – but one calm afternoon without a whisper of wind, reading in his cabin, Sandy opened his porthole and caught the unmistakable smell of peat smoke. He went on deck and seven miles away lay the coast of Ireland: 'Pretty good smelling! Only possible after thirty days of Atlantic gales.'

*

At midnight, returning from patrol for coaling, the *Mantua* ran aground on an outlying bit of Scotland. Everyone was at their station in three minutes but it was low tide, the ship would float off in a few hours and unless caught by a submarine there was no danger: only the eerie silence of a dead ship stranded on a rock. Next day they hobbled up the Clyde to dry dock where it was found that repairs would take a month. It meant leave for the whole ship's company.

Sandy went for a few days' fishing on Loch Awe. Out in a boat with only a light trout rod and no gaff he hooked something big. The line shrieked off the reel; the boat was towed all over the loch. At one moment Sandy jumped ashore, hoping to pull the fish on to the beach, but it raced off like a torpedo, Sandy tumbled back into the boat and took up the chase. Eventually, after shouting to an old man ashore for a gaff, a thing like a shepherd's crook was brought out. At the fish's first kick lying in the boat the gut cast snapped – one more rush would have saved it. The fight had lasted an hour and a half, the fish weighed twenty-two pounds: 'How is that for my first salmon?'

Next day, with another officer, he drove through some of the grandest highland country where the whole world seemed at peace. Neither of them gave a thought to the war till the evening when they heard that the Germans, after publicly warning of it in New York, had sunk the transatlantic liner *Lusitania*. 'What unspeakable devils they are! But after their diabolical gas attacks can one be surprised at anything? Do we still believe the enemy is honourable and a gentleman?'

Back in Glasgow he got an order 'forthwith' to join the *Agincourt*, the navy's biggest Dreadnought battleship, at Scapa Flow. He said goodbye to his three friends in the *Mantua* – 'curious how one gets attached to a ship, even a floating

HMS *Agincourt*

barn, but she had been my home for nine months, longer than any house for many years' – and after the easy-going ways of a merchant cruiser he was nervous of the plunge into such an unnatural habitat. But on hearing that the new doctor had come aboard armed with a rod the commander invited him to go fishing, ending with a farmhouse tea – 'eggs, scones, butter, honey, like the old days' – and Sandy was almost reconciled. Ten days later, after watching rows of warships at anchor as if they never moved, his initiation was complete: 'By Jove,' he wrote, 'I wish you could see the grand fleet steaming majestically over the sea! It is one of the finest things I ever saw.'

One by one battleships, cruisers, destroyers, slipped through the gate in the antisubmarine net and took up formation, turning and wheeling as well-drilled as guardsmen, keeping station with miraculous precision. 'The most tremendous exhibition of power ever seen,' Sandy called it, 'and it brings a lump to my throat.' The *Agincourt* was more than twice the length of King's chapel – 'Think of it!' – and a double line of them could perform a hundred-and-eighty degree turn at twenty knots in perfect order. The little destroyers were just as impressive, circling the fleet at speed, dashing off to anything that might be a submarine – 'generally it is a whale' – and returning to heel like good dogs. If the British navy was as good at gunnery as at ship-handling, Sandy decided, the German fleet had better stay at home.

But the likelihood of battle was remote. Sandy chafed at his idleness while army doctors in France were toiling day and night for the wounded. 'I hate war and all things naval and military more than most people, and this has spoilt my plans for life. But I could never look myself in the face, nor anyone whose opinion I valued, if I did not carry on as long as I was wanted. Afterwards, heaven knows... ' Meanwhile he could poke quiet fun at the navy's love of trivialities – the angle of a sailor's cap, the width of another's trousers – and make the most of fishing trips with the commander or a picnic when officers went off in boats to a lonely Orkney cove, to bathe, scramble over the cliffs, collect driftwood for a fire, boil a vast iron kettle, fry eggs and sausages. Too soon it was time to pack up and get back to the ship.

The *Agincourt* was sent to Portsmouth for a refit and Sandy was admitted to the Naval Club, 'a good old house with a notable cellar', where he dined in comfort and passed happy hours in the library. During a few days' leave he squeezed in a visit to Cambridge, with lunch at King's. Only a handful of undergraduates were in residence, half the buildings were occupied by nurses, the college had lost more men than any other for its size. One of them was a young climber who had walked into battle with a revolver and an ice axe, never to be seen again: 'When all these good people are going it is hard to sit in the security of a battleship.' All day in Cambridge it poured with summer rain; he wished he hadn't gone.

In the second winter of the war the *Agincourt* was back in Orkney where the hills were white with snow and it was too rough to get ashore. Time slid by unnoticed, Sandy wished it would go quicker, grudging every wasted day. To keep sane, in touch with nature however domesticated, he grew hyacinth and crocus bulbs in his cabin. Then early in 1916, after seven months in a battleship, he was dug out at short notice and found himself on the way to the tropics – medical officer of a naval landing party in German East Africa. 'They are going to put sailors and guns ashore, and some idiot told the Admiralty that I knew all about that country and its diseases. It is too funny, but I won't undeceive them... It is a tremendous stroke of luck, just the thing to suit my peculiar tastes and experience, and I ought to get some fun out of it – if I know anything of sailors. I shall be more useful there than with the grand fleet and may even see some fighting.'

On the ship to Cape Town the general in command – known for his victories on the racecourse and polo field as much as the battlefield – became seriously ill and asked Sandy to continue looking after him in South Africa before he was invalided home. Later he wrote to tell Sandy's parents how grateful he was for their son's devotion and skill: 'The simplicity and honesty of his character made him a very pleasant companion, and it was with a sincere regret that I left him behind.'

*

Ten years after landing at Mombasa, on his way to Ruwenzori, Sandy was back there, taking the train upcountry again. Near the British-German frontier he joined a detachment of marine artillery in scrubby country with Kilimanjaro in the distance, 'the glorious mountain which the Germans have no right to – we shall take it from them.' They moved south to the war front where Sandy was soon in battle, excited by the sight and noise of heavy guns firing at a German position on a hill, followed after dark by an infantry attack. It was what he had wanted years ago, first in the Boer, then the Russo-Japanese war, but now he found his enthusiasm tempered by seeing the bush set alight by gunfire and native villages burnt.

The East African campaign became a string of running fights as the dwindling German force, driven back from the coast, was chased across Africa – outnumbered by the British but led by a master of guerrilla warfare. After each battle, despite heavy losses, the German survivors got away to fight again till the last remnants, living off the land, slipped over the frontier into the swamps of Portuguese territory. It was clear that if the original British general had been in command, instead of his bumbling replacement, the enemy would have been quickly mopped up and the campaign finished.

Sandy was kept close to the action, moving steadily south as the Germans were pursued in an exhausting cat-and-mouse game. The country was hardly worth fighting for, he thought, 'but it will be a great thing to turn the last German out of Africa.' And he hoped for a chance of climbing Kilimanjaro before the show was over, whenever that might be: 'I don't think the Germans can last many months. They might hang on in small parties, it is a huge country and difficult to traverse, but they have been cut off for so long I doubt if they have much heart left for anything. But give the devil his due, they are fine fighters.' Dead oxen, mules, horses, littered the roads, camps were foul and stinking, the rains turned the world to mud, the dry season filled it with dust. Five months after starting, when his marines had advanced two hundred miles down Africa into the heart of the German colony, Sandy was attached to a Rhodesian unit too; later still to a squadron of the Royal Flying Corps. Malaria and dysentery were deadlier than the enemy: 'Our people go sick in thousands and die by scores, so the likes of me are kept busy and fit.' But he didn't enjoy army company, the battleship *Agincourt* had been far more congenial: 'There were people there whom I liked greatly, but here there are none whom I take to much.'

It was something he tried to correct in a letter to his mother: 'I am sorry you have the impression that I don't like people – that is quite wrong. I have found many people here that I like and many I am sure who like me, but one does not make many new friends at my time of life, especially in circumstances where people come and go so quickly, and die or are killed. I have learnt to like people whom in the past I should have taken no notice of. Indeed, I find most people have their good points and I honour them accordingly – especially those who show their better side in these conditions. No one knows – and no one probably will ever know – what the rank and file have had to put up with in this campaign. But that is a censorable remark and one of the reasons why my letters have been so bald.'

He was getting 'rather mouldy' – perhaps a relapse of the malaria that began in Africa, pursued him to New Guinea and was to trouble him for years – and found an excuse to go down to the coast, to Dar es Salaam and across to Zanzibar where he walked through gardens of cloves and ate fresh fish and oranges, a blessing after months of ox meat and no vegetables. He smelt the sea again and was entertained aboard a naval ship, an antidote to the petty bickerings of the army: 'I have learnt something of the two services since the war began and bow my head to both, but I shall always be glad that a chance word at dinner at the Savile sent me to the Admiralty rather than the War Office.' Soon he was back 'in pursuit of the errant Hun… We are about ten-to-one but still he slips away. The end is certain, but the cost is great.'

Early in 1917 the fighting reached the Rufiji river, with the enemy on the far side. Then the advance across the river began: 'Awful scrimmage for the next few days. Much work with wounded and sick.' As the Germans retreated south, fighting all the way, the British pursued them and Sandy was put in charge of a small river steamer, the *Hyacinth*, bringing out the sick and wounded – a job straight out of Joseph Conrad. The river was in flood, the country lay underwater with scattered huts raised on piles, the people travelling in dugouts: 'Except for the heat and the strong current it is not unlike the Norfolk Broads.' The voyage upriver was straightforward with little work for a doctor, but a hundred miles inland they picked up a shipload of casualties to be brought down to the coast: men packed like herrings amid noise and smell – Sandy's hands were full. On April Fool's Day, piling on the agony, the *Hyacinth* got stuck on a sandbank: 'What wouldn't I give to be back in England! There must be primroses and violets and chiffchaffs at home.'

Later he took charge of evacuating casualties, British and German, from small ports along the coast up to Dar es

Salaam; and finally he was made port medical officer at Lindi, close to the frontier of Portuguese East Africa. There he set up a drainage scheme to reduce the havoc of malaria, and acquired a little dog Sally, an unclaimed passenger off a ship: 'Such a little dear, full of life and very fond of master – I can't think what I have done all these years without a dog.' A bigger astonishment was hearing that he had been awarded the Distinguished Service Cross: 'For what I cannot imagine unless it is a prize for being the oldest naval surgeon.' The official citation was, 'For conspicuous devotion to duty and for his unfailing care of the sick and wounded during operations in East Africa... In the Rufiji river delta he voluntarily attended to the casualties of the river transport service in addition to those of his own unit.'

The last Germans were driven out of East Africa but Sandy felt out of touch with the world. Newspapers came two months late, the Russian revolution in 1917 was a distant rumour. So was any chance of peace: 'Wouldn't it be better to stop it now before more death and destruction? I can't help thinking the mass of Huns are as tired of it as we are.' In March 1918, more than two years since coming to East Africa, he left Lindi on his way home. But first he would stop in Kenya, at Lake Naivasha again, 'the most beautiful place in the world – indeed even more beautiful by contrast with the hideous places I have seen these two years of war and by its perfect peacefulness... I could wish to stop for always. The birds and beasts swarm as ever, the mountains and lake are beyond words beautiful. I can shed more than twelve years and find myself back in 1905, sitting on the sunny slope of the island where willow-wrens sing in December as perfect a song as in an English woodland in June. I could have bought this island then for a thousand rupees if I had had so much. Now the owner refuses eight thousand pounds and is likely to get ten thousand. What an opportunity lost!'

Three months later he was home and on leave, fishing in Wales: 'No fish but very pleasant. I walk about and get wet and am happy so long as I can forget what I go back to in a fortnight. How I hate the prospect of it all!'

*

The war was fizzling out; Sandy was sent on special service. In the summer of 1919, six months after the armistice – four and a half years after loading gold into the *Mantua* at Arkhangel – he was back there, caught up in an international venture to save the port from capture by the Bolsheviks, the terrible 'Bolos'. For a week before the ice melted, they cut through the White Sea. Seals lying in thousands on the floes, seal pie for dinner, the creaks and groans of melting ice, the bitter cold and midnight sun – it was a glimpse of the arctic which Sandy was glad of, but enough to show he had done well to avoid polar expeditions. And he wasn't pleased to be cooped up in a ship again, 'but I have been mighty lucky to have kept out of it so long.' Though he was sad to miss another English summer there were rivers and forests with redstarts, white wagtails, oyster catchers, tufted ducks, even a swallow, to rejoice in. But while the golden onion-topped churches of Arkhangel looked picturesque from the Dvina river, the streets were stinking bogs ending in rubbish dumps and the infinite tundra.

He was more impressed by the arrival of the military force, five thousand bemedalled veterans marching on to the stage like an opera chorus. Their general was presented with a large cake and a bowl of salt by anti-Bolshevik White Russian dignitaries, but nobody seemed to know what it was all about. In white tropical uniform, in a fickle climate of extremes, Sandy joined the staff of the naval force in a flotilla of gunboats sailing far up the Dvina, exchanging long-range shells with Bolo gunboats. Neither side scored many hits. It was hoped to drive the Bolos back and eventually get through by river and lake to Petersburg, more than a thousand miles away. But the channel was mined, the water level fell, the White Russian troops were hopelessly incompetent. Forests of birch and pine – and swamps breeding a plague of mosquitoes – were full of northern birds, but Sandy could never get ashore; and though he had brought his rod the nearest to any fishing was when a mine exploded in the river, throwing up a splendid geyser, killing a lot of fish which were grabbed by the ships' crews.

The operation seemed pointless, an exercise in pure confusion, and news of the outside world was scantier than it had been in East Africa. Sandy supposed they were serving some useful purpose, but it was hard to see it without knowledge of the murky, shifting Russian situation, and 'I wonder who has that?' If it were not to condemn Arkhangel to the mercy of the Bolos, 'the best thing we could do would be to clear out and leave Russia to mind her own business.' For several weeks the flotilla bombarded a town far up the Dvina: 'Tremendous attack… We got everything we wanted except the Bolo gunboats which escaped upriver. We took over two thousand prisoners and practically all their land guns, so they are not a very active force now.'

But the river was now so low, there was no hope of getting through to Petersburg; and even doubt about the gunboats returning to Arkhangel and the coast: 'It would be very ignominious to have to sink them here and go downriver in barges.' In the end – the end of a semi-comic but futile coda to the war – they got out into the open sea and Sandy sailed for England.

Five years after walking into the Admiralty he walked out of it, a civilian: '*Laus Deo*!'

V Mount Everest

'If you know a war profiteer who wants to support geographical exploration,' Sandy wrote in 1920 to a likely friend, 'please introduce me.'

He was glad to be home though doubtful if he would stay long: 'I do not find myself in tune with the people of this country. Many things jar, but I suppose that is bound to happen. My only salvation would be if some bold lady were to attach me to herself as permanent bodyguard, but no one shows an inclination for it. The alternative is New Guinea, whither I shall return if I can scrape up the means.' His hopes for a third expedition were blocked for lack of funds. He tried rich individuals as well as institutions, but the war seemed to have taken everyone's money. He was an explorer in a blank world without a job.

A literary friend compiling a popular book about famous explorers included Sandy, who didn't feel he deserved it and wrote to say so: 'You would put a pygmy among the great ones of the road, and he is not fit to be seen in such glorious company.' A climbing friend writing a manual of mountain craft asked Sandy for a chapter on the tropics – 'You are the only real explorer alive' – and was given some useful hints.

'Don't laugh at the natives, but learn their greetings and submit to any ceremony of blood-brotherhood. They are quick to take advantage of the smallest sign of weakness or favouritism, and one should establish a scale of barter – one bead for a sweet potato, say, or a fish-hook for a spear. Medical treatment is a sure way of winning respect, and castor oil works wonders where verbal threats or bullets are of no avail. Camping by a river, the Europeans' tents should be pitched upstream of the natives'.

'In the early morning when leeches stretch themselves expectantly on every twig, a wise man walks in the rear of his caravan; any that attach themselves should never be pulled off, even from the most intimate parts, but with a touch of tobacco juice from a well-smoked pipe they will shrivel and drop off. For snakebite a ligature should be promptly applied, tightened with a stick, relaxed every half-hour to avoid gangrene, and the whole area cut away with a sharp knife and washed with permanganate of potash. Boils should be treated with boric acid before cutting off the head and applying a drop of carbolic. For coughs and colds a mustard bath is advised, and a dose of Dover's powder – 10% ipecacuanha, 10% opium.

'As to food, variety is important but all tins taste the same – meat or fish or fruit – though after months of beef and mutton a jaded stomach welcomes jugged hare or curried prawns. Raisins or figs or ginger can counteract the flavour of tin, and some people crave for pickles. Teeth are liable to loosen or fall out, and a sufferer from toothache may prefer extraction at the hands of an amateur to the horror of prolonged pain. A small glass of whisky before supper relieves the monotony and assists digestion, and a cup of cocoa is a comfort at bedtime. Brandy is for emergencies and champagne for the convalescent stage of malaria. As to headgear a wide hat lined with red cloth, with protection for the back of the neck, is best, but if a pith helmet is preferred it should be covered with waterproof material or it becomes sodden with rain. A mackintosh cape is useful in camp and barber's clippers are invaluable, with spare umbrella, shaving tackle, inkpot, watch-glasses. Never take anything you can do without but take everything you may need, especially books, and leave things behind when they can no longer be carried. Finally, when in doubt – boil.'

Such an unpompous man must have smiled as he made the list. He may have enjoyed giving advice, the hardened explorer passing on his wisdom, but at forty-five he didn't consider himself a retired explorer and though a schoolmaster's son he was never a pedagogue. He would prefer to be out there in the jungle himself.

Then ironically – unexpectedly, delightfully – he was elected to a six-year fellowship at King's, at the heart of the academic world. It was a bold, imaginative tribute and he felt deeply honoured; also amused at what King Henry VI, the saintly founder of the college, would say about a Kingsman with only a pass degree being made a fellow: learned in the far places of the earth and in his knowledge of men and things, but an undonnish don. His range of experience and friendship would be unique among scholars with narrower lives, without his vigour, his restrained charisma. 'Charming fellow,' one of them remarked sniffily. 'Knocked about the world a good deal, I hear.'

Soon Sandy was busying himself, not just in college life but in the buildings and gardens and the trees along the Backs. Defying the conservatives' outcry he set about grubbing out and replanting; and turned in particular to the fellows' garden where trees and shrubs were packed in among plants 'that have no business in anybody's garden. It is astonishing how much the beauty of a place is enjoyed and how little is done for its future.'

Astonishment came in multiples. Sandy had hardly settled into King's when, early in 1921, he was invited to join the first expedition to Mount Everest as doctor, naturalist, botanist. The leader was a rich Irish colonel, the climbing party was to include Mallory, in modern legend the figure most closely associated with the compulsion to climb Everest, 'because it is there'; last seen in 1924 with his companion vanishing into the mist, 'going strongly for the top'.

*

All that was known about Everest was that it was the highest mountain in the world and nobody had climbed it. It straddled the frontier between Tibet on the north and Nepal on the south, two secretive countries whose rulers preserved their lands from intrusion. Unlike Kanchenjunga, showing off its splendour to anyone in Darjeeling who stepped off their veranda, Everest was shy, modest, hiding behind other peaks almost as high as itself. Nobody had seen it closely, it was just a point on the map fixed by triangulation from the distant plains of India. A few Tibetan monks, shepherds, traders, flogging their yaks and mules over the high passes, were aware of it – 'Goddess Mother of the Snows' – but the idea of standing on top was ridiculous, also blasphemous. Then early in the twentieth century xenophobia seemed to be melting and two British officers, viewing Everest from sixty miles away in Tibet, thought they saw a possible approach. But the Great War put a stop to such frivolity.

After the war ambitions stirred again and in 1920 – the Year of the Iron Bird – the Dalai Lama gave permission for an expedition to enter Tibet. A committee of eminent geographers and alpinists met in London, the novelist John Buchan was enlisted to handle publicity, the King and the Prince of Wales smiled graciously. It could be a new jewel in the imperial crown, it was anyway to be a first-class operation with a distinctly military flavour. 'To climb the mountain', the chairman, an old general, announced, 'was to be the first object and the mapping and everything else was to come afterwards... The topography, the fauna and flora are of very small consequence.'

Sandy could never share such bigotry. But the expedition included surveyors and a geologist as well as climbers, and the plan in 1921 was to reconnoitre the whole region – its valleys, glaciers, lesser peaks – and make a dash for the summit if there was a chance; but to return the next year for an all-out assault. To Sandy the penetration of a mysterious corner of the world promised more than the bagging of a peak, and with a naturalist's and botanist's collecting outfit added to his medicine chest he joined the huge party at Darjeeling. The Europeans – 'sahibs' for the occasion – would be carried on ponies, their baggage on a hundred mules. It wasn't Sandy's style of travel, more raj than rough-and-ready. But on the first stages of the journey when each day ended not with pitching tents in heavy rain but in a government bungalow, he decided it was perfectly agreeable: 'You just walk in and find furniture, knives and plates, lamps and oil, even a library of old magazines and novels.' With luck there might be wild goose eggs for breakfast. And to show his observant eye was uncorrupted by luxury he added, 'Cardamoms cultivated here.'

From the start he was enraptured by the trees, plants, animals. The long ride up to the Tibetan plateau lay through forests blazing with rhododendrons of every shade and size, wild roses, poppies, primulas, orchids. Over a stony pass in cloud, the Tibetan frontier, then into another more European country with oaks and walnuts and anemones. Even the sky, when the sun dissolved the clouds, was a familiar blue, not the colourless filtered sky of India. That evening at supper in the bungalow a vase of flowers on the table would stir the most phlegmatic sahib, though several stomachs had gone wrong – cooking was difficult at that altitude and their cooks were 'unspeakably bad', usually drunk. Next day the ponies had 'a nice scamper' among grazing yaks and goats, then up through birch and juniper woods into a lovely valley, 'better than I have seen in the Alps', with a stream rushing between scented cherries, pale irises, strawberries in masses: 'It is impossible to exaggerate the beauty of the scenery and vegetation.' There were trout in the pools, caught by Indian porters in their hands and by sahibs in butterfly nets. And birds – dippers in the stream and a chough, a hoopoe, larks, even a cuckoo. And swallowtail butterflies, and 'a jolly little fat tailless mouse' in swarms, vanishing into burrows at the travellers' approach, and herds of wild asses and gazelles. By a lake Sandy watched a red fox stalking a pair of geese, and 'had the satisfaction of saving the birds and spoiling his game.'

After two weeks of bungalow-hopping they left the traders' road and trekked across open country, pitching tents on the bleak Tibetan plateau. But Sandy, escorting one of the sahibs whose dysentery needed treatment at a mission hospital, profited from a detour down into Sikkim. 'A wonderful change to come from the dry plains and hills where almost nothing grows to this streamy valley of trees and flowers. The air in Tibet is fine and exhilarating... But it is not my country and I don't want much of it. There is nothing beautiful in huge snow mountains rising out of a bare plain, and I am not even sure there is any real beauty in a snow mountain pure and simple.' But he relished new experiences – hot yak's milk and Tibetan tea infused with salt and rancid butter and even a few spoon-fuls of tsamba, the bane of Himalayan travellers, a porridge of mashed barley mixed with tea: 'It filled a gap and we did not starve.' Making friends easily, grateful for their hospitality, he slept in a ragged tent of yak hair with twenty Tibetans: men spinning and weaving or praying at a simple shrine, a woman churning sheep's milk into butter, singing as she worked, another stoking the yak-dung fire, filling the tent with bitter smoke – all creating an atmosphere 'about as beastly as it could be... But every night has its end,' and Sandy, as far as possible from the dons' common room at King's, savoured the unlikeliness of it all.

Back on the high Tibetan plain he rode as hard as his pony would go to catch up with the rest of the expedition, camping in the governor's fort, a tumbledown affair of mud and brick, and entertaining the inhabitants who came to stare and stick out their tongues to show pleasure: 'I see a large number of fat pink tongues daily.' On the whole he found Tibetans 'friendly but greedy for money – they are indescribably dirty and beyond words ignorant and superstitious.' He had no time for such religiosity, the shrines and images everywhere, the huge monasteries full of monks in idle meditation or turning wheels and waving flags, extorting wealth from hard-working peasants. The governor had orders from the Dalai Lama to help the travellers but stop them killing any living creature – a blow to Sandy who had already shot two larks for skinning and a pigeon for supper. But Buddhist precepts must be observed, anyway near a monastery or one of the countless hermit's cells.

Then on across the wide plain in brilliant sun, still mornings with freezing wind all afternoon, sometimes a sandstorm. Such stark landscape didn't suit Sandy; he would have been more at home in jungle. It was a pity, he told his mother, that there was no artist among them, for any beauty lay in the skies and lights which a photograph could never catch. In fact his own photos were some of the finest brought back.

At Tingri Dzong, a month after leaving Darjeeling, he found the expedition based in an old Chinese barracks, a place of unimaginable filth where one by one the porters, 'vile in their habits', collapsed with typhoid. Sandy was left to tend the sick and dying and make collections of animals and plants, mindful of Buddhist feelings, while the other sahibs scattered in small parties to discover the country. Everest was fifty miles away, Mallory and another climber had gone to examine the northern approaches. To Sandy it looked 'quite unclimbable, it is so terrifically steep'. But a note came from Mallory to say they had climbed a peak of over 23,000 feet. 'Good – but it doesn't make it any easier for me to stay kicking my heels in

The Everest Expedition, 1921: Sandy is standing in the back row, far left; Mallory is seated in front of him; and Col Howard-Bury, the leader of the expedition, is the man in the check jacket, on Sandy's left

this beastly place.' He was an explorer first, then a reluctant but always scrupulous doctor.

The colonel, leader of the expedition, came back from Kharta, closer to Everest and better for a base: a valley of flowers and wild gooseberries to make Sandy impatient to move on. 'How I should like some fresh fruit and vegetables!' he wrote to his mother.

*

Two weeks later with another sahib, 'a very nice fellow', Sandy got his chance for the kind of travel he loved. From the plain they climbed steadily beside a rushing river to a pass at 18,000 feet, the highest Sandy had been. A bridge washed away by floods was being rebuilt by peasants while a man blew hideous blasts on a conch shell to keep off the rain. Sandy, pleased that sorcery didn't work, noted that it rained heavily all afternoon. Further into the mountains, in a valley of barley fields and golden mustard, he found gentians and blue poppies, parnassus butterflies, twittering long-tailed marmots – things to lift a naturalist's heart; and occasionally a lammergeier, the noble bearded vulture, swooping from its cave on some remote precipice to fix a gleaming eye on the intruders. Some of the world's grandest mountains rose ahead and Sandy began to appreciate the scenery, especially the alpine flowers – edelweiss, blue aconites, dwarf rhododendrons; and brushwood fuel to cook on was a pleasant change after weeks of yak dung. But a village dog stole a marmot's skull drying outside his tent and the governor, a slippery man in a silk gown with long fingernails to show he was above manual work, forbade the sahibs to trade with his people and hastened them on their way, deceiving them about the route ahead.

With one yak and a gang of Tibetan porters, male and female, they struck out into country no European had seen. Over a high pass, camping by a river while the Tibetans sheltered in caves – but the cook failed to light a fire with green rhododendron sticks, making Sandy yearn for 'some of my good Dyaks' who could make a blaze out of the wettest stuff. Next day they travelled through a valley of great sanctity where rocks were painted with the prayer, *om mani padme hum* – hail! jewel in the lotus – and where every bush carried a scrap of cotton fluttering a message to heaven; where shrines were plastered with butter, filled with pilgrims' flowers; where chanting monks burnt incense and dumbly accepted offerings. They came to the temple of Lapche dedicated to a saint who once lived under a rock and whose footprint, planted there before he was carried to heaven, was still worshipped. It was hard to believe that this squalid building reeking of butter-lamps, its walls set with hundreds of prayer wheels for pilgrims to turn as they plodded round and round, was one of the holiest places in the Buddhist world. And it was maddening to see unfamiliar birds, animals, even butterflies, and be unable to collect them for fear of offending someone's transmigrated soul.

Sandy's own enlightenment, unholy but supremely joyful, was in the discovery of an unknown primula: 'It has four to six bells on each stem, the size of a lady's thimble, of a deep blue colour and lined inside with frosted silver' – an exquisitely rare plant now named *Primula wollastonii*, available on the internet from specialist nurseries.

In bad weather blowing up from Nepal they crossed two high passes, traversed glaciers, stumbled over moraines into a valley where the flowers at their feet made up for the lack of view. But when the mist cleared they were treated to a vision of one of the most superb Himalayan peaks – Gaurisankar, rising into the sun from woods of birch and rhododendron, thrusting a knife-edge blade of ice to the blazing summit. The sceptic was converted: Sandy now saw beauty in a mountain 'pure and simple'; and ten years later his photo of it, taken with a big plate camera, hung in our Cambridge house.

They travelled on through valleys heady with the scent of roses, and over passes, skirting the northern satellites of Everest. The people, 'much given to religion' with wind-machines and water-wheels busily praying for them, were happy to sell an ox or goat, but it had to be driven far into the distance to be killed. A herd of gazelles, confident of protection, came to watch the sahibs pitch their tents in a grove of willows. Half a life ago wild deer on a sacred Japanese island had fed from Sandy's hand. Now the search for natural history specimens had brought him, an unwavering atheist with a distaste for all religion, to a very different holy place at the other end of Asia.

The monsoon had broken, it was cold and wet. They slogged on, blinded by rain and hail, and after two-hundred-and-fifty miles through unmapped mountains reached the expedition's new base at Kharta, twenty-five miles east of Everest.

*

Sandy and two others went for tea with a Tibetan landowner in his house among junipers, willows, poplars. A tent was pitched in the garden, they sat on stools covered with carpets, a feast was brought: peas in the pod and raw rose hips for a starter, then junket with pea flour, bowls of hot milk, macaroni and minced meat spiced with chillies, potatoes and a wild fungus from the woods – a trial for the sahibs' skill with chopsticks. Afterwards their host brought out an old stringed instrument, a banjo with a carved horse's head and two sounding-drums, which he played 'not unmusically' while singing Tibetan love songs. The words amused everyone else, but nobody would translate them for the sahibs. It was like those African canoe paddlers on Lake Kivu long ago, singing rude songs about their passengers.

Monsoon clouds driving up from the south left knee-deep snow on the mountains, making high climbing impossible. Mallory and his climbers were frustrated, they should have been up there weeks ago before the monsoon broke. Now they must wait for the weather to clear, when days and nights would turn freezing cold. Sandy, who I suspect had misgivings about Mallory's drive for the goal, was thankful not to be with him in the sterile heights; there were riches enough for a naturalist in the valleys towards Nepal.

Trekking with the colonel down into a hotter, greener world – through gorges, along mountain streams into woods of birch, sycamore, alder – Sandy thrived on all that was missing higher up: plants and creatures to be collected in the further-ance of knowledge. The colonel noted Sandy's enjoyment of it all in 'surely the most beautiful valley in the world... Nothing was too small for his attention – the birds and flowers, the marvellous scenery unrolling before us day by day, the glaciers descending among tall fir trees.' Even the leeches were old friends of Sandy's though the porters, seeing him slice them in half with scissors, thought he was doubling the number. They passed down the valley into a softer land of butterflies and birdsong where villagers, never having seen white men, brought them cucumbers, pumpkins, red currants, honey cakes. Then up to a pass with a low wall of stones and turf marking the Tibet-Nepal frontier. On the far side lay a pretty lake with rocky islands, a perfect Scottish loch – there were sure to be fish in it, Sandy thought wistfully. But it was forbid-den country, a Beyond he could never reach.

At night, sitting outside the tent by a fire of juniper logs, he watched sadly but stoically as moths died in the flames instead of in his killing-bottle. Next day he and the colonel returned the way they had come, toiling back into the high mountains. 'Tibet is a fine spacious country,' Sandy wrote. 'Plenty of sky and colour, all on the grand scale. I am glad to have seen it and the Himalayas. But it hasn't stirred me as some other countries have.'

At Kharta there were signs of autumn – barleyfields ripen-ing, willows turning yellow. But the weather still prevented high climbing and there was little time to make a bid for Everest before winter was on them.

*

Mallory and his climbers had explored all routes and believed that an approach – the only one for porters with heavy loads – lay from the valley up the Kharta glacier to a pass, the Lhakpa La, then across the East Rongbuk glacier and up steep rock and ice to the North Col of Everest. If they could set a camp there for two or three acclimatized sahibs, the final ascent up the north-east ridge to the summit looked straightforward.

Defying the last rumbles of the monsoon they set off to put an advanced camp near the foot of the Kharta glacier, and a few days later Sandy and the rest followed. For the first time in three months all eight members of the expedition were together, imprisoned in their tents by the weather with deep new snow on the glaciers. To Sandy it was deadly monotonous – 'the wonder is that we don't all bite each other's heads off' – but while the others played bridge he found new birds to collect and sometimes a solitary lammergeier wheeling royally, enviably, far above. Some of the party climbed a lesser peak, though Mallory and others were exhausted at the top, 'which does not look well for our Everest attempt'. But what Sandy, as doctor to sahibs and porters, feared most was frostbite at high altitude. Already on the Kharta glacier it was cold enough by day and bitterly so at night.

The altitude affected everyone with lassitude; the next stage to a higher camp at 20,000 feet had to be taken slowly. But sometimes the clouds broke, revealing across the glaciers a panorama never seen before: the ice cliffs and fluted snow ridges and rock crests of Makalu, the immense tumbling precipices of Chomolonzo, and Everest itself, formidable, ringed by hanging icefalls, dwarfing the assembly of unnamed, unimagined mountains round it. It was a privilege to be there: to be granted the first sight of giants waiting a million years in secret glory for these Englishmen to come and look.

*

It was time – if not too late – to make an attempt on Everest. With twenty-six porters Mallory and five sahibs, including the colonel and Sandy, left the camp at four in the morning. 'Down to the glacier, and there we put ropes on the coolies to keep them together… Then began a long trudge up the glacier. The moon, nearing her last quarter, gave plenty of light at first, then dawn at about five-thirty. Crisp snow and a gentle ascent for two miles – all quite easy. Towards nine o'clock the sun began to get very powerful, the snow softer, the ascent steeper. At about 21,000 feet we saw curious tracks like those of a small man walking fast and easily. Coolies assured us they were the tracks of one of the wild men, a small people covered with hair. My notion is that they are the tracks of a wolf loping along at just the pace to make its four feet give only two tracks… Going now became difficult and the heat on the glacier almost intolerable. The difficulty of lifting myself up a few steps at a time was as much as I could manage, so how the coolies carried thirty-pound loads I cannot think. Somehow we all did it, and by midday arrived at the col we were making for. I was nearly the last, but going well enough. In the matter of colour we were all about equally blue.'

This was the Lhakpa La, 22,350 feet, at the head of the Kharta glacier, a howling place cut by winds, from which a steep descent to the East Rongbuk glacier would lead to the North Col and perhaps the summit. At sunset they crawled into two-man tents, a struggle in their breathless state, and swallowed a little thin soup, cold ham, biscuits; then settled down for 'the most beastly night'. Sandy didn't think much of this heating up of tins and melting of snow by the sahibs – they should have brought a cook with them. The temperature fell below zero, the snow underneath grew into bumps and ridges, only Mallory got more than a snatch of sleep. In the morning they managed half a cup of lukewarm tea and iced sardines dug out of the tin. Boots were frozen solid, Alpine clothes – tweed jackets and puttees with too few sweaters and socks – couldn't keep out the cold. When Sandy tried to take photos his fingers froze to the camera.

Decisions had to be made. Mallory and two climbers with a few porters would try to reach the North Col, then look for a way up the north-east ridge. The rest would retreat to the lower camp and wait for their return. Sandy was thankful but cautious: 'We were all very stupid and muddle-headed and took rather a time to get off. I do hope they will all come back none the worse for it... Got down as fast as we could to our camp which seemed like the height of civilization... Tea extraordinarily good.' After the exertions it was a pleasure to loaf about in idleness, out of the cold, but from the top of Everest great plumes of fresh snow streamed into the sky, showing what the climbers could expect up there.

Two days later Mallory and his men returned, one having suffered signs of frostbite. From the Lhakpa La they had pitched a camp on the East Rongbuk glacier and next day kicked a way up ice and snow to the North Col, to be met by a savage gale. It was their limit, they could get no higher. Though Mallory said he could have gone on, the others were knocked out by such ferocious weather, and they came down. Now they crowded into Sandy's tent for 'a relieved and cheerful evening – a tight fit but it made for a little warmth.'

*

Sandy was glad to be leaving the heights. There was endless country to travel through, undreamed-of valleys and passes to explore. Within a week, on a grassy plateau, he was 'camped with great contentment, and breathing with comfort... Woke to one of the most perfect mountain days to be imagined. Breakfast in hot sun outside the tent, then away collecting seeds.' Next day in a meadow he lay on a bed of rock roses and ate his lunch: 'A most heavenly place, and I watched the tops of Makalu coming and going in the drifting clouds.' At the other end of the Himalayas in the 1950s, when famous peaks were being knocked off one by one, I found pleasure in country known only to shepherds, climbing nameless mountains that, probably, nobody has since visited.

Sandy and the colonel camped on a lawn blue with gentians, travelled down a valley, across hills and streams, past a lovely lake among meadows of irises. But autumn was on them and when they got back to Kharta the barley had been harvested, the trees were full of red and gold. A curlew calling in the night told Sandy he was on his way home.

'Our time here has been extraordinarily interesting,' he wrote from Kharta, 'but rather a picnic compared with New Guinea. I don't know that I ever want to come back. My chief delight has lain more in the indescribable beauty of the flowers and the sight of these mountains, than in the conquest of Everest itself.'

The trek back across 'the vile Tibetan plain' became a race against winter: dodging snowstorms, struggling to knock tent pegs into the frozen ground, collecting seeds of plants he had noted in the spring. Then down from the plateau to an almost tropical country of parakeets and small green oranges, further down through forest and rice paddies, back to Darjeeling more than five months after leaving it. 'Got rooms at the club and had lunch with admirable beer.'

He reached England in December 1921 – too late for Founder's Day feast at King's, 'a thing I have been looking forward to for months.' But a few days later 'I hung up my hat, as they say, for the first time in twenty-five years. Since I ceased to be an undergraduate in 1896 I have lived in lodgings or tents or ships, and have had no place to call my own. So this is quite a pleasing experience.' He sank happily into it, and the following spring wrote to his mother, 'What a lovely country England can be when it likes. Here the trees and grass are about at their best... What do you think of kingfishers and goldfinches nesting in a town like this? Nightingales are still common, but I have to listen very intently to hear them from my window.'

In London a great Everest meeting was held at the Queen's Hall at which Sandy was due to speak on medical aspects and natural history. But the colonel was followed by Mallory who went on too long, and the Duke of York was beginning to yawn, 'so the meeting broke up and my quips were wasted.' He was asked to go back to Everest in 1922, the first serious attempt on the summit, but declined – 'wisely, I feel sure.' He didn't care for another 'bandobast', a massive assault, and probably saw that the 1921 reconnaissance would remain the most enjoyable of all Everest expeditions. Nothing in the future – not even victory – could have the same enchantment.

VI MARRIAGE AND BEYOND

In biography, it seems, there is an element of autobiography. A private engagement between two lives. A pattern of parallel experience, mutual humanity. I can only understand my father by looking into myself. By observing my own behaviour and transposing it to him – or vice versa. By watching what I know of his life and assessing it in the light of mine. By guesswork, intuition, conjecture, based on particular facts picked from a bewildering store, an infinity of evidence. Am I being fair? Am I drawing his portrait as I believe him to be, or only as I should like him to be? Would people who knew him recognize it? Would he see himself in it? I should love to ask him.

In the remote places where he explored Sandy suffered a craving for music. Though his mother was a fine pianist she was too impatient to put up with her son's struggles with the violin and he didn't get far. 'I never enjoyed music so much before,' he wrote after a recital by the great violinist Joachim. 'It makes me mad to think what a fool I was to give up playing the fiddle when I was a boy. Who knows, I might by this time have played quite respectably, and I haven't the courage now to begin all over again.' In 1906, coming down from Ruwenzori to Entebbe, he found 'a little German clerk playing on a shockingly out-of-tune piano. It was the first music I had heard for ten weary months and I made him keep it up till midnight, when his hands were worn out. He hadn't much execution but the true spirit of Beethoven, which put me into such an "ecstasy of joy", to quote Mr Pepys, that I couldn't sleep.'

It was through this craving that he met the woman he would marry. In 1911, back from his first New Guinea expedition, he went to a concert in the Queen's Hall. An old King's friend was there with his wife who said to her husband afterwards, 'I liked that man.' He was invited to their house and introduced to one of the wife's many sisters. Sandy was thirty-six, Mary Meinertzhagen twenty-two. Did he remember the young girl, also fourteen years younger than he, who had tried to teach him to dance on a ship crossing the Indian Ocean?

Mary was ninth of ten children, possessed by almost as fierce an independence as Sandy. As a young woman before the Great War she had travelled – sometimes with a brother, often alone, always perilously – in Russia, the Caucasus, Armenia, Kurdistan. Unlike Sandy's scientific quest, hers was idiosyncratic, literary, romantic. She spoke French, German, a little Russian; and while Sandy took Pepys and Conrad and Kipling on his journeys, Mary read Blake, Ibsen, Virginia Woolf.

Some months after their meeting, packing for his second New Guinea expedition, Sandy summoned the courage to invite her to tea. She wrote that she would love to have come but was going away, and sent good wishes for his adventure. He was 'horribly disappointed, but I had a sort of idea that some-how or other you would not come... I don't mean that I thought you would try to get out of it, but that something would prevent it. You haven't missed much in the way of enter-tainment, for nobody has been to tea with me except an occa-sional man about once a month. Never a woman, or lady or girl – what a pity there is no word corresponding to man – and you would have been a new and very delightful experience to which/whom I was greatly looking forward. You will think me an awful idiot but I know so little of people, apart from men, that I never dreamed it was even possible to ask you to come to my den, and now I am consumed with regrets when I think you might have come – or rather, I might have invited you which is not the same thing – several times in the months that I have been living here. But then I didn't know you lived in London and were barely, if at all, conscious of my existence. What a rotten life it is, and how confoundedly short... I spend half my time saying goodbye to people I never see again... I am still so ignorant of you that I do not know if this is an impertinence, but I will take the risk: if ever you are bored with civilized life and want to talk to a savage, a letter to me will be greedily wel-comed.' And he went back to New Guinea for another year.

But across the world he wouldn't lose touch. From a dirty little port in Borneo, recruiting Dyak porters, he wrote that he had seen a magazine article by Mary about her travels in the Caucasus and was bold enough to congratulate her: 'It is curious how much better you know a person when you read anything he/she has written. I have found out all sorts of things about you that I did not know before, but I am sure there were other things in the part of your diary you suppressed. I should like to read that too, but I don't suppose you will ever let me.' He may have thought of his own writings where he gave away so little of himself, and turned to something more fanciful: 'I wish we were not so conventionally civilized, and you could transport yourself on a carpet to these parts and accompany me on my wanderings. I know I should see twice as much and get twice the pleasure that I do alone, but perhaps you would not get quite the fun out of Malays and Dyaks and Papuans and the other queer people I have to deal with as you do from Kurds and Georgians and such folk... By the time this gets to you, you will no doubt be off on some journey to the other side of somewhere, and I shall imagine you sailing down the Euphrates or getting captured by brigands. I hope not.'

Over the next twelve years they seldom met or even wrote. In the Great War, when Sandy was in the navy, Mary joined the Land Army and drove a team of carthorses on a farm. In the winter of 1914, patrolling the North Atlantic in the *Mantua* with men separated from their homes and families, Sandy wrote to a friend's wife: 'Seeing the sad state of some others, I have been glad these last months that I have no wife and children.' Perhaps he was being disingenuous.

From the *Agincourt* a year later he wrote to Mary, 'I have

often wondered where you were, and if I had to make a guess I should have said Campden Hill. Somehow it sounds wonderfully peaceful and remote from war, and I should dearly like to be within hail of it, though the people who live up there always make me so dreadfully shy... If as you say your family colony attracts Zeppelins, Campden Hill must be a more lively place than it used to be... Last July when I had a few days' leave I should have greatly liked to see you, had I known where you were. As it was I spent a few days in the country, and you can imagine how sweet the good earth smelt after these months at sea... Naval officers, though jolly fellows, know only their own kind and their own job, and this becomes rather tiresome... We talk war, war, war. Damn the war – forgive me... It has become a horrible obsession. I do not think people of my age will outlive it. I was forty last May and am entitled to speak like a grandfather... It is extraordinarily pleasant to hear that there is still music in the world and that you have been to hear some. How I should love to do the same. One begins to shrivel up mentally and morally, and it is good to be reminded that in spite of all this foolishness and horror there is some beauty.'

After the Armistice in 1918 Mary did relief work in Poland with a group of Quakers, and in 1921 Sandy went to Everest. From Darjeeling, packing baggage for the mules, he took 'the last opportunity of writing to you before we get into Tibet. There is a glorious view of Himalayas from here, and I have seen glimpses of Kanchenjunga towering over the clouds... I am sure Everest will not be half so fine. I wonder what riding on yaks will be like. Are they all they are said to be in *A Bad Child's Book of Beasts*?'

He was provoked by something Mary had said: 'In spite of being "a strange man of some twelve years' acquaintance" I am going to write to you if you do not think me a bore. I think you are dreadfully unapproachable, for you have so much family and you all know each other and your friends so intimately that a stranger has no point of contact. And you live in London where everything is so unnatural. I can – at least I think I can – learn more about a person under the open sky than in all the drawing-rooms of London. But I am really a savage at heart and hate crowds and cities... You say that some day you will use a pickaxe on me. Well, I take it rather as a compliment, implying that you would like to know more than my physiognomy. I wish you would try it, but I can't guarantee you will find anything worth finding. When you begin to pick you must make allowances for the abnormal life I have led in uncivilized places, where I have had to be content with the company of men... I wonder what I really seem to be to you? Probably a forlorn old buffer – I shall be forty-six this month – with an interesting past and a very uncertain future. That is a pretty accurate description. The future is what frightens me... Enough of this stuff – and may all good be with you.'

Five months later at Kharta, after hearing from Mary, he

replied, 'If you often write letters that give as much pleasure as this you deserve more than a crown of glory. It reached me a fortnight ago in a high-up camp where we were snowed up for days, and did me a world of good. I like to be told to shut up when I talk rot about my age, and I very much like to be liked, so if this is the kind of pickaxe you threatened to use on me, please go on with it and you may make something of me in time. Talking about age, I admit, is a silly affectation, for I don't feel old a bit and get as much joy out of life as ever I did, and so may it continue.'

In Delhi at the end of the expedition he took time to 'inflict another scribble on you, from a more civilized place than the last, though I am not sure I wouldn't sooner be there than here. For now I am playing at being a globetrotter and it is not a success, as I am a wretched sightseer and generally avoid show places. I once spent a week in Venice without going inside St Mark's. You will think me an awful philistine and perhaps I am, but wandering about Indian cities alone is a deadly amusement. I would give anything for a congenial companion. Indian buildings, so far as I have seen, are fearfully overrated, not to be compared with the Moorish buildings in Granada or Seville. Their arts and crafts are beneath contempt. Perhaps I must not damn them utterly as I have not yet seen the Taj Mahal. After that I am going to make a beeline for Peshawar and the Khyber Pass, which attracts me much more than all the tombs and ruined palaces in India. You will think I am in a nasty discontented frame of mind, seeing no beauty in things that people would give their ears to see, but I am really in rather a nice kind of mood – only hating the restriction of houses and cities. No doubt I shall get used to them.'

*

Back in England in 1922 he still hoped to take a third expedition to New Guinea and was trying to collect funds. Meanwhile he could enjoy his fellowship at King's, a place to entertain his friends with the resources of the college kitchen and cellar. Wherever he went he brought the gift of meeting people at their own level – an Italian duke or a Dyak headhunter, the captain of a battleship or a gardener – and now he could extend it to a professor of history, a famous zoologist, a brilliant choirmaster, the college servants and an endless number of undergraduates. Young people in particular, even children, became friends. Across the generations, through their eyes, he saw a future different from the obvious, the inevitable, the boring: a future lit by an explorer's vision. With him there was unique excitement in climbing a tree, hunting for a nest, breeding a caterpillar and marvelling at the butterfly it hatched. A woman in her ninetieth year remembered, as a girl of six or seven, walking with Sandy and her father in the New Forest. They came to a great old beech with a low branch springing horizontally from the trunk. A hardly spoken pact passed between child and middle-aged man. She climbed on to the branch and slowly walked along it towards Sandy at the other end, fixed by his intense blue eyes willing her not to lose balance while he gently bounced the branch. More than eighty years later she could still see those eyes inspiring her with a magic in adventure she never lost.

Another man's child… But what memories would lie ahead for his own children when they appeared – if they ever did? One of the saddest things about his early death was to be deprived of memories still to come, the ones that never happened. All my life I have missed his future and his part in mine.

His friends saw in him a natural godfather for their children. 'You pay me the highest compliment and I accept with pride,' he wrote on being asked to take on another goddaughter. 'But you know I am a very unsatisfactory person and am not likely to be of much help to her, either in things spiritual or material. But as I go tottering down the solitary years she will be growing up and will perhaps come sometimes and see me!' He was indifferent to the baptismal aspect but loving, unorthodox, always interested. Perhaps he cared too much. And recently, soon after Everest, he had been shattered by the death from pneumonia of a favourite godson: 'He made a manful struggle but was beaten last Tuesday, three days after his sixth birthday. He was the most lovable child and we trusted each other uncommonly. It is a bitter blow and a proper punishment for keeping the love and trust of a child and taking none of the responsibilities. I have been so wrapped up in my own affairs that it only just begins to occur to me that I have made a mess of things and missed the best in life. I am still a bit bewildered.'

It brought him to another discovery: an unknown Beyond waiting to be explored.

*

In 1923 he asked Mary to marry him. She refused, and in the opinion of one of Sandy's few woman friends she lost the chance of her life. He was less certain: 'She would have found me a mighty difficult problem. All the same, I have not given up this quest and do not intend to until I have been knocked down flat again. She came with me to a theatre on Tuesday, so I am not entirely excommunicated.' A week later he told the friend, 'I am afraid it is utterly hopeless. We had dinner last night and talked it over and inside and out for three hours. She likes me very very much but says she could never get to care for anybody in that sort of way, so it seems there is no more to be said. Unfortunately I care a good deal more than I thought. It is a bitter business, like one of those dreams where you suddenly fall through space with a sickening bump. But I suppose there is a purpose in these things. I wish I could believe that, or could know what the purpose is... Next week I hope to take the road to Scotland.'

He had lived always for himself; it would be hard to change his ways. Though not a 'confirmed bachelor' with undertones of deviancy, his chosen solitude had only been broken by male colleagues on an expedition or in the navy. Now, failing to raise money for New Guinea, he faced another sadness: 'My affairs do not prosper in the least. My Mary and I spent a heavenly day together this week. She loves to be with me but she does not love me, so we have said goodbye until she finds she wants me, which I am afraid will never be. It is a rotten business and makes me very wretched. I suppose I ought to see a funny side to it but I can't – yet.' One of Mary's sisters told her she was a little fool. One of Sandy's oldest friends, Charles Rothschild, deep in his own melancholia, refusing to see a doctor, turned the key of his door and 'put an end to himself in a most horrible way. It has been an awful shock and is constantly in my mind... I owe almost everything in the world to him... There are four children.' To escape, hearing of unexplored mountains in Colombia, he changed his plans and was impatient to get away. Soon he would be out of reach, doing what he loved best.

Then suddenly, a fortnight before he was to due leave for South America, the clouds lifted, the Beyond lay open: 'I believe I am going to find happiness.' At a restaurant with Mary he talked of Colombia. She wished she could go with him. Only as his wife, he said, and she decided she did love him: 'She doesn't yet know how much or why or in what way. If I were half a man I would pick her up and carry her off to the nearest parson or registry office, but I think all will be well. It might conceivably happen that she will sail with me. Wouldn't that be great!' A week later it was fixed: 'I can't tell you how happy I am… I was going to be a crusty old bear, and now I am never going to be anything of the kind. Mary loves me and I love her – isn't it too glorious! I find it difficult to think about anything else – selfish pig I am.' To another friend he wrote, 'Don't think it was a sudden inspiration. But you wouldn't if you knew her. I am beside myself with happiness. Think of me, at forty-eight! The world is turned upside down. "Poor old boy," you will say.'

With no time for second thoughts they were married almost furtively in King's chapel. Sandy had once written to Mary, 'I have loved the college and chapel more than any other spot in the world. From the beginning King's became a new home for me.' Though he wrote books and articles about his travels and won medals and honours, and his name was given to a mountain in Africa, a kind of Tibetan rabbit, a tree frog and a pipit and a bat from New Guinea, a Himalayan primula and a giant African lobelia and forty other plants, and fifteen butterflies and insects, he told her, 'I have been more proud of being a member of the college than of anything else in my life.'

He had hardly mentioned his family and Mary only recently learnt that he had a brother and six sisters. After their marriage he took her to meet his parents for the first time – a short day's visit was enough for him, they didn't stay the night – before boarding a banana boat in Hull. Even now, crossing the Caribbean, he couldn't ignore the scientist in him: 'In latitude 13° North I saw Venus with the naked eye at 2.10 p.m., half an hour beyond its meridian – bright sun and very clear.'

*

For a honeymoon Colombia was a severe testing-ground. From the port of Santa Marta they endured a stormy passage along the coast in a schooner, living in two dog kennels on deck, both prostrated by sickness – 'altogether the most poisonous voyage I have been on.' Landing at a decayed little town, a hotbed of pearl-poaching and rum-smuggling, they were examined for contraband and cheated over the price of mules; and were 'mighty glad' to slip away in the middle of the night. Keeping to the coast, they rode through alternate mangrove and thorn scrub, crossing rivers by canoe with the mules swimming alongside – 'pelicans along the shore, a few cranes in the swamps' – and next evening reached a village. 'Very hot and tiring day', Sandy noted, 'but Mary as happy as I am, so all is well.' They bathed in the river, watching out for crocodiles, and were visited by half the village who turned out to see them eat supper.

Two days later they started inland, with six oxen for the baggage, two Indians, one half-Indian, a woman with a baby on her back, a child driving a pig, a dog and themselves on mules. Soon the oxen bolted and smashed the loads, Sandy was thrown from his mule, and they had to return to the village. Setting out again, they rode for days through a tangled land of bush and muddy lagoons infested with huge horseflies. It was a relief to reach the sparse shade of the Sierra Nevada

Mary, on honeymoon in Colombia

foothills, but insects were still bad and they spent every evening outside the tent, pulling out each other's ticks before a swim in a mountain stream. It was a lifeless land – an occasional parrot or humming-bird, few butterflies, only three flowers worth noting – and the people were no better: puny, thieving, superstitious, too drugged on coca or drunk on sugar wine to be any help to the travellers. 'Their worst failing,' Sandy decided, 'was their masterly indolence.' But Mary was happy, getting out her penny-whistle when the Indians played their reed pipes. They hadn't seen a white woman before and were convinced by her long hair and breeches that she was a boy – the honeymooners were father and son.

They rode on over ridge after ridge of dense forest 'like

Ruwenzori', climbing ever higher to a point near a snow peak of 17,500 feet. Sandy wanted to cross the range and the prospect looked good, but it was too steep for oxen, the porters refused to go further. Food was hard to find, Sandy and Mary got ill with hunger, they gave up exploring and returned to the coast. There was an uneasy moment after pitching the tent by a river when they went for a bathe by lamplight and Mary swam across to the far bank, heedless of the crocodiles Sandy had seen upstream. She swam back safely and next day, riding through a brighter, livelier country of birds and wild oranges, 'we satisfied our hungry bodies with beer and a fairly good lunch.'

In great discomfort – in mutual delight – they had travelled through hundreds of miles of unknown country, leaving much to be discovered and mountains to be climbed.

*

On their return they looked for a house in the West Country – 'where the rivers flow into the Atlantic, no other sea will do,' Sandy insisted – and settled at Bencombe on a steep Cotswold hillside. In the four years they lived there I believe – I must believe – that it was bliss for them to be alive. Though Sandy was fifty and Mary nearly forty, they walked hand in hand through the garden like young lovers at the beginning of the world.

I was born at Bencombe in 1926, the middle of three children, with a sister on either side, but my chronology of that early childhood is vague. I ran down the field through waist-high summer grass and battled in the winter snow, laughing then crying for the cold. I stood on a chair to stir the Christmas pudding, I sat by Mary while she read a story, I rode upstairs at bedtime on someone's back – Sandy's, I suppose. In the morning I slipped into their enormous bed where I could see Sandy's shadow through the door, shaving in his dressing-gown. He, or his shadow again, played with us on the terrace while Mary with her pocket-folding Kodak stepped out the distance heel to toe, then turned to shade the viewfinder and squeeze the rubber bulb. I look at those photos now and find them poignant but oddly unconvincing. Can that be me, with fat little legs and a sunhat? And is that really Sandy, whose presence in my life has been more vivid than the middle-aged man, familiar though somehow strange, snapped for ever one distant happy afternoon? More telling is the tiny scar I see in the mirror near the corner of my nostril, a memento of the day when, running down the path with a wooden flower label in my hand, I fell and stuck the point into my nose; and screamed. I screamed all the way to the doctor's where Sandy held me while stitches were put in, and went on screaming till he bought me a clockwork steam-roller and stuffed a cloud of lavatory paper into the funnel for smoke.

I can smell the mothballs behind empty clothes in the cupboard on the landing. I can see the brass telephone in the hall with a winding handle for calling the exchange; and the engine in the stables to make electricity, driving a belt that cracked like a whip; and the stone balls along the garden wall. I can hear the whine of our car going uphill in low gear. As a bachelor Sandy had had an old Dodge tourer with canvas hood and cellophane windows. Now he bought a modern Austin Twelve, a family saloon, and taught Mary to drive. A pony-trap took us to the village shop, an adder lay coiled and basking in the sun, a sparrowhawk stole one of our doves, foxes killed the chickens, a pair of goldfinches nested in the quince tree.

Sandy, with Georgina and Nicholas, at Bencombe, April 1928

'I was simply wonderfully happy in those years at Bencombe,' Mary wrote to a sister long afterwards. 'I can't tell you how perfect our life was, day after day, so much so that I thought it can't go on like this, and I wondered how I could love any man as much as I did Sandy.' He too was in love and, on hearing that Maynard Keynes, a fellow of King's, was to be married, sent congratulations: 'In the last few years I have found my life immensely widened – it was not exactly in a rut before – and have gained an undreamed of happiness. So I can guess a little of what lies before you.'

But Mary was right – it couldn't last. Their bliss was cracked on the 'fateful day', as she called it, when Keynes came to stay bringing an invitation. Sandy's fellowship had expired but the college wanted him back, to live in Cambridge and be college Tutor. Everyone agreed, he was exactly the man to get on with the undergraduates.

Sandy and Mary talked it over. At first Sandy was reluctant; he couldn't bear to break up their idyll. Mary said yes, but they were only living for their love and the children, and there was more in Sandy's life than pottering about the garden. Perhaps she knew that if he refused the offer from King's – an older love in which she had no part – a bitterness might steal into their marriage to mar the perfection. Perhaps she saw there was one more Beyond calling him from further than the Cotswolds. A horizon is merely the limit of one's vision, and both Sandy and Mary were far-sighted people. In the end he accepted – it was a compulsion he couldn't deny – and a month later went to Cambridge.

'This comes straight from heaven,' he told a friend, 'and I hope I may not be found wanting. The uprooting will be hateful, and separation from my family before we are installed elsewhere will be damnable – but these are small things in the long run.' Was he being callous? Selfish? 'I am too young to be doing nothing at fifty-three… It is a big adventure again, but what has my life been but one adventure after another? And I have been simply dogged by good fortune.' Adventure was what fired him. And good fortune dogged him till the very end.

He began work at King's early in 1929, while looking for a house for Mary and the children, all under five; and found he was happier than he had ever guessed. His job was to interview undergraduates, advise them on their courses, hear their problems, generally be their friend and counsellor. He made himself accessible, keen to lend his insight, his understanding of the human condition, and was soon one of the best-known, best-loved dons. Questioned for a student magazine on his academic degree he confessed, 'No, not even a third – but they wanted someone used to dealing with savages.' It was a refreshing attitude, endearing him to almost everybody.

Fitting into 'the rather difficult community of college life', he told Mary, wasn't easy for him. But if he felt some prickliness among the stuffier dons, he did his best to take the junior common room's point of view. 'I know something about every one of you,' he said to an undergraduate who left his rooms feeling he had been talking to a man who wanted to listen and knew when to encourage, when to dissuade. And another, in bed for ten days with flu, was visited first thing every morning by the Tutor – who was, after all, a doctor too.

Echoing what he had once said of Dyak porters he wrote, 'I like the young men and really believe they like me... They are a queer mixture of assurance and shyness – but all human and friendly.' The secret lies in a remark by Keynes, who called Sandy 'a man to whom it was unusually easy to speak the truth, who could unlock hearts with a word and a look, and break down everyone's reserves except his own.' But he ached for his family and told Mary so: 'I simply long to come home – and damn all these rotten college meetings... The sun has shone all day and the daffodils are just perfect, yet you know, dear heart, how I wish I were home with you. Today I must waste a lovely afternoon sitting in a room discussing fellow-ships.'

Alone at Bencombe during the university term, with three small children who went to bed after tea and nobody else to talk to – surrounded by all that reminded her of life with Sandy – Mary's happiness languished. They put the house on the market but there were no takers, and Sandy couldn't find a house in Cambridge near King's.

A year passed, Mary begging him to come home more

often, but he was so busy, it was such a distance, he couldn't fit in trains to be back for work. Tormenting herself, she began to believe he could come if he wanted, and surely the college would show sympathy. When she went to stay with him in a Cambridge hotel she found him so tied up with work, she felt a twinge of resentment, even jealousy. He had a purpose in their separation, she had none and returned to a sort of false widowhood, seeing her husband only at rare weekends and in vacations. Sandy would be remembered by a generation of Kingsmen as the perfect Tutor, a bitter-sweet truth for Mary. It was as if his call to King's had been a curse on her.

When I myself turned up as an undergraduate, the porter touched his bowler hat and shook my hand, proud to meet Sandy's son. But I was proud of nothing except a private hope to make my own way, though in the end I got a degree no better than his.

Sandy tried to cheer Mary with his letters: 'How lovely to see the geese flying over Bencombe. It makes one doubly glad to be alive to see such things. But you are such a long way away and I keep thinking what you are all doing... However Time does move and the frost will soon be out of the ground. It seems as if the earth were softening a bit already and crocuses will soon be in flower... Candidates for exams in and out of my rooms all morning. Such nice lads – I really do like these young ones. It is a heavenly day – sun shining, and the window by my writing-table wide open for the first time this year. But why am I not in the garden at home with you?'

He too was often lonely, despite his work, and felt stranded. He tried reading modern novels – D.H.Lawrence, Hemingway – but was lost, even disgusted, and went back to Conrad and W.H.Hudson. He would borrow a car and escape into the country or slip into King's chapel for evensong, though he was never a believer. 'My darling heart, I wish you had been with me in chapel... Some wonderful music – Dowland, Byrd, Bach's *Come Jesu Come*.' He looked forward, he told Mary, to taking the children there as a rare treat. Meanwhile, 'You can't think how much I long for Saturday, with you and home and our three little pigeons – and I shall smell the good smell of West Country earth, and perhaps I shall have green gooseberries!'

Eventually he found a house three minutes' walk from King's back gate, to rent at eighty pounds a year. Mary went to see it, and at Bencombe she drew a picture for us. It had a hole in the garden big enough to get lost in, and I imagined a mine shaft. Bencombe was sold but the new house wasn't ready, so Mary took a flat near Notting Hill Gate, close to her family and friends and Kensington Gardens. It was the time of Christopher Robin and *When We Were Very Young* – which was what we were. We went to the Round Pond and the statue of Peter Pan; and then in the early summer of 1930 Sandy met us at Cambridge station. Beside him in the Austin I put out my hand to turn into the gate, recognizing the house from Mary's picture. There was a fire bell on the chimney, green shutters, a stone terrace in front. But the hole in the garden was a grass bowl that might once have been a fish-pond or gravel pit. Laughing with excitement we rolled into it till bedtime, and later every year we had our Guy Fawkes bonfire in it.

It was a month before my fourth birthday. I keep one more elliptical vision of Sandy during the next two weeks, the last of his life, when he lifted me on to his knee and helped himself to more quince jam.

∗

Sandy's killer was called Potts. I know his other name, but simply Potts is enough to define him in my mind. Brief and stark, it suits his stunted life. In June 1930 he was nineteen when he shot two men, then turned the pistol on himself and pulled the trigger once more. But he would have died any-way, condemned for the double murder if not reprieved for insanity.

For me it became a short story, melodramatic but plausible, with near-fictitious characters I invented. Mary shielded her children from the events and all we knew was that our father was dead and our mother was crying when she came down to breakfast. She said nothing about the shoot-up till she thought we were old enough for it. I was ten when she told my elder sis-ter and me one evening, abruptly getting up from the sofa to stand at the mantelpiece with a handkerchief. She turned to kick the coals so that we shouldn't see her tears, and as well as rage at losing Sandy so cruelly I felt a kind of privilege. I could cry too, it was something we had in common – not so much that she was crying like a child but that I could cry like a grown-up. I also felt a touch of superiority because she was telling me something I already knew. A boy at school had blurted it out: 'Your father was shot by an undergraduate, wasn't he?'

I denied it: 'No, he wasn't.' Sandy had died, that was all. Not that he was less real for being dead – he was just different from other boys' fathers. His presence, made of facts and figments, was what I loved above all. I knew him dead better than I had known him alive; he now lived as he never had before. But the manner of his death was no part of the myth, and to discover it might kill my most cherished treasure. The other boy had the tact not to argue, though without saying more he showed that he knew better. And from the way his words worked like grubs in my mind, I came to believe them. So Mary's secret had been kept to no purpose. For me it was a time of dissolving darkness, emerging consciousness, and I should have learnt the lesson: never to save something for a better moment without being sure nobody will get there first. But often, like missed chances, there have been things I have put off, only to find it was too late. 'In delay', Don Quixote said, 'there is usually danger.'

Later, when I was sixteen and Mary also died, I found an envelope of Sandy's obituaries which she had kept. One in the

Church Times ended with sympathy for the bereaved and a hope that Sandy and the policeman might rest in peace – also the young murderer 'who most needs our prayers'. It drove me wild. Let the villain roast. Nothing was too terrible for the man who had left me without a father, who had broken so many lives one afternoon when all he need have done was take his own. But in time my feelings changed from rage to indifference, finally to curiosity. I grew to recognize a strange, tenuous connection with Sandy's killer, as I do with my characters in a novel.

Potts had come to Cambridge with a scholarship and a reputation for being unusual, and in the summer of 1930 was at the end of his first year. I can see him clearly: slim, pale, debonair, his hair smoothed back, a college scarf round his neck. He played the drums in a jazz band, the Blue Melodians. He hired a piano, he ran up debts. His friends were mostly in other colleges and nobody knew him well at King's, where he was both obscure and conspicuous. He was clever, nobody denied, but he may have felt the need to cut a dash. You didn't forget him, they said, once you noticed him. He wore polo-necked sweaters, scarlet or canary yellow, and plus-fours with check stockings like the Prince of Wales. He verged on the theatrical and dressing-up was part of the act. Sometimes he wore a false moustache or took a more flamboyant name.

Now he was in a mess. At home in the Easter vacation his father had settled several unpaid Cambridge bills, but after he went back for the summer term nothing was heard for six weeks, till a letter came from the Tutor. Potts was absent without leave, Sandy wrote, nobody knew where. The police were told; but, though unaware of it, they had been given a clue when an undergraduate in another college reported a missing pistol. He had bought a Webley automatic to take to South America after leaving Cambridge. Early in May it was gone.

Potts had stolen it. He showed it to Newman who played the trumpet in the Blue Melodians, and suggested a life of crime together. In a borrowed car they toured village pubs, earning a little money on the piano and trumpet, cadging more. To anyone who would listen, Potts claimed to have royal blood, to own fifty suits, to have his life insured for twenty thousand pounds, to be heir to the principality of Alsace-Lorraine and entitled to be called Prince Lorraine. At least one girl fell for it and thought she was engaged to him. It was the good life, far from lectures and petty rules. Sooner or later the two would be expelled from Cambridge, but they couldn't stick it anyway. They applied for passports, they would go abroad. And they bought a motorbike.

But the clouds were collecting. Pressed for the return of five pounds he had borrowed Potts telegraphed half the money and Bolton, a friend in Newman's college, lent the rest. Soon they were desperate; they must pay their debts or get out. Before the university caught up with them they would ride the motorbike to London and sell it; and in the last week of May they drove away, swearing that nothing would drag them back. In London they got twenty pounds for the bike but it was Saturday, they couldn't cash the cheque till Monday. They drifted through the West End and slept on the steps of St Martin-in-the-Fields. Masters of their fate, young, free, they didn't mind living rough for a time. When the bike money was gone there would be something else to sell or someone to borrow from. Till then they wandered the streets, sharing fantasies, sleeping out.

Five days down-and-out were enough. They needed drama, glamour, company, to match their dreams. On Thursday night when it began to rain Potts remembered an address someone had given him. A flat in Shaftesbury Avenue where Madge Miller lived. After midnight, wet and tired and dirty, they rang her bell. Twenty-five, auburn, petite, Madge worked at a nightclub, calling herself a dance instructress: a figure from fiction with a heart of gold, 'no better than she ought to be'. She wasn't surprised to be knocked up in the early hours by young men-about-town with money to spend, though these two were broke; and she put them to bed in her spare room. It was the start of a very lost weekend. The clichés, like the clouds, were closing in.

Next morning Potts spoke of a man at the Savoy Hotel who would lend them money, and he and Newman went off in search, but had no luck. Perhaps the man was a character in a Potts story. Potts pawned his cufflinks, bought horn-rimmed glasses and false whiskers, and had his hair waved and dyed ginger – as a disguise or to play the dandy. That evening they took Madge to the movies and a restaurant, ending with a music-hall. Potts paid till his money was gone, then Madge stumped up. It was raining again, they went back to her flat to play poker for matches. There was nothing else to do.

Over the weekend Madge, who wasn't a silly girl in a village pub, learnt a little of what was going on in Potts' mind. At Cambridge he would be arrested for a smashed car and he pulled out the gun: 'If the cops come for me I've got this to show!' Madge told him not to be a fool. He boasted of another warrant for fraud over a loan from the heir to the Russian throne. But Madge knew about romantic young men; he ought to go back and face the music. In defiance he cried, 'If anyone comes through that door I'll shoot myself.'

'Not in my flat, you won't,' Madge said.

On Saturday, a week after their flight, they pawned a watch and chain; and Potts wrote to Bolton, who had paid off his loan, asking for his dress clothes to be sent from Cambridge – to sell or to wear, he didn't say – addressed to a false name at poste restante, Charing Cross. That night, after Madge had borrowed more money, they went to the movies again. On Sunday, leading them through the empty city, Potts pointed out his father's office; he had never seen it before. But on Monday Madge put her foot down. She had a job to do, she turned them out. Potts and Newman drifted for another day and night. Dossing down on the Thames embankment – the place for tramps, the plot was wearing thin – Potts waved his pistol over the river, revelling in the hunt. He swore the police wouldn't get him, Cambridge would never see his face again.

On Tuesday they went to Charing Cross to collect Potts' dress clothes. But Bolton himself was there. He had told his college about Potts' letter and would try to bring them back by car. Newman was soon persuaded; it took longer with Potts. He was in a fright – this was no part of his fantasy. Action was what he wanted but he didn't know his lines, he was drying up. In the end, after ten days on the run, he agreed to go with them. On the way he said, 'I feel I'm putting my head in a hornet's nest.'

Bolton, who didn't know about the gun, said, 'Cheer up – it won't be so bad.'

*

It was June 3rd 1930, two weeks after we had moved to Cambridge. That same morning, by chance, Mary took an early train in the other direction on a cheap day-ticket to London.

Though for a fortnight she had been living in a place where she had no friends and which she would never grow to like, she and the children were back at last with Sandy. At first she had believed that life was going to turn out as perfect as at Bencombe, but it hadn't happened. Sandy's work filled his day and he was expected to dine in hall, then stay late in his college rooms for any undergraduate who came to see him. Often in the evening Mary was alone again, still half of a divided marriage. She knew Sandy would have loved to be with her; knew too how her mood affected him. He tried to show her their life must now be different, but nothing could dispel the sense of doom that haunted her: a vague fear that nothing would be quite right again. She felt it that morning when Sandy drove her to Cambridge station and told her of his worries about an undergraduate who had disappeared – 'a bad lot' whom the police also wanted to question. 'Oh Mary my darling, do kiss me!' he called as she got out of the car and hurried to the train.

She was a Londoner at heart, she looked forward to her day in town. She would do some shopping, see one of her sisters, perhaps go to a gallery. But the strange curse had followed her. She went to Harrods to buy things for the new house, but seeing a cousin in the distance she left, she didn't want to talk to anyone; didn't want to answer questions, make explanations. She had lunch alone and went to the Leicester Galleries in Leicester Square. There was an exhibition of modern prints – Gauguin, Van Gogh, Matisse, Lautrec – and in a happier state Mary might have bought one, but today she could summon no interest. And again, catching sight of two friends whom she would otherwise have enjoyed meeting, she kept away. She was restless, impatient, troubled for no reason she could tell. Her life seemed somehow spoilt. Had she spoilt Sandy's too, this last year since his return to King's? But no, he had been as loving as ever, delighting in his new adventure. She would wander about till there was a train back to Cambridge.

Also that day – in a twist of surrealism – Charles Rothschild's widow got a letter from Sandy which caused her acute distress. It mostly concerned a visit to her which he was planning with Mary, but it ended, 'Yesterday while strolling across Newmarket Heath I was once again joined by Charles, who walked over the downs with me.' Nothing more, just a bald statement. It was seven years since Charles Rothschild had killed himself. Yet here was a man not known for psychic encounters – except for the strange case of his *doppelgänger* in the New Guinea jungle – claiming that yesterday he had been walking on Newmarket Heath with Charles.

'Wollaston has gone off his head,' Mrs Rothschild cried in alarm. To her, Sandy had always been an honest atheist, even a harsh one, unwavering in his scepticism for religion or spiri- tualism or life after death. 'But look at this!' She showed the letter to her daughter Miriam and they scrutinized it with incomprehension. Sandy's writing was small, hard to read, but the word 'Charles' was clear enough. What frightened them was the matter-of-fact tone as if Sandy wasn't surprised to meet the dead man; and 'once again' suggested that it wasn't the first time. 'Collectors are unusual people,' Miriam, herself an eminent naturalist, wrote years later. But Sandy didn't elaborate or even say if Charles had spoken to him or they had walked together in silence. And Mrs Rothschild, my god- mother who sent us a hamper from Fortnum & Mason every

Christmas, never had a chance to ask. Later that afternoon Sandy too was dead.

*

In Cambridge at midday Bolton and Newman drove to their college, leaving Potts to walk to King's alone. His feelings – resentment, ignominy, pride – would remain his secret. What he didn't know, though he must have guessed the stolen pistol had been reported, was that he was being followed through the town by a police detective. Trumpington Street, King's Parade; then by chance he met the man who was the very one to go and see – the Tutor, a man of whom another undergraduate at King's wrote later, 'It was possible to go and tell him things and ask his advice as if he were a father.' As indeed, he was mine and my two sisters'.

The meeting was fatal to both men and to the third who was watching them. The players were moving into place for the last scene, one turning killer, the others victims. What Potts and Sandy, reckless prodigal and resourceful explorer, said was never known. Together they went through the gate into the college. In the words of that other undergraduate, if a reprimand was needed Sandy would offer it 'in the kindest, most straightforward way, man to man'. And though reticent himself, he could draw out the intimate thoughts of others. But he was an uneasy agent of authority, indifferent to the trivialities of discipline. Long ago he had wished he could make himself unpleasant but failed, and must have dreaded this interview.

'Men *took* exeats in my day,' he would tell undergraduates who came for permission to leave Cambridge.

His rooms were on the ground floor of Gibbs' building, the classical block across the front court next to the chapel: the building from which, in a wartime dream at sea, he had watched bombs falling on Cambridge. Behind tall windows he had a big outer room facing the court and two smaller rooms, a bedroom and study, overlooking the great lawn down to the river and the Backs. Somewhere over there, across the bridge, beyond the trees, was the house where his children were having lunch; where that evening he would stroll in the garden with Mary and hear about her day in London. 'You might justly say that we have all that we deserve,' he had written to a friend, hoping for a visit. 'We are fortunate people and the most unlikely things happen to us.' Now, at half-past one on a summer afternoon, fortune was taking the unlikeliest turn of all.

A few minutes later Detective-sergeant Willis called at the porter's lodge with a warrant for Potts' arrest and was directed to the Tutor's rooms. Sandy, talking to Potts in the study, came into the outer room to meet Willis. 'You'd better go in and see him,' he said, and they went back into the study. Unaware of danger – it was a lovely day, he would go for lunch in hall afterwards – Sandy stood by the empty fireplace while Willis arraigned Potts. The three were close to each other in the small room. But hardly amicable. It was all over in a minute.

Willis cautioned Potts, told him he would have to come to

the police station to be charged, and began reading out the warrant. Potts didn't let him get far. The first bullet hit Willis's shoulder without much damage. Willis struggled to get at Potts and push Sandy aside to save him, but fell over a chair. Potts fired twice at Sandy, then again at Willis. Finally, for which everyone later must have been thankful, he fired at his own head.

Mortally wounded, Willis lay trying to remember how many shots he had heard. He kept still, afraid that Potts might have another bullet. In time he looked up and saw Potts lying near the fireplace, his head in a pool of blood, with Sandy beside him. Willis got to his feet, staggered through the outer room, reached the door above the front steps. 'Help!' he called, sinking to the ground. The head porter ran across the court to his aid. 'He shot me – I shall be dead in ten minutes.' But he lived sixteen hours, long enough to tell the story.

The quiet of King's College was broken. A man who had explored unknown lands and reached the top of unclimbed mountains, who had lived through fevers and tribal attacks and a long war, died by a crazy bullet in a secluded Cambridge precinct: 'the chance and innocent victim,' someone wrote, 'of something like a South American shooting affray.' To many people, ironically, Sandy became better known for his appalling death than for his distinguished life. To me, it meant I lost a father and gained a myth.

The news rocked the college and raced through the town.

Before the end of the afternoon it reached London. Coming out of the Leicester Galleries to catch a train home Mary saw a terrifying headline across the evening paper:

UNDERGRADUATE SHOOTS TUTOR DEAD:
AMAZING DRAMA AT CAMBRIDGE.

She almost fainted. She knew it was Sandy but had a queer feeling that if she didn't read the paper it wouldn't be true. Blindly fumbling for a penny she gave it to the man.

'Read all about it,' he said. And she did.

***

If my father, Sandy Wollaston, had had to choose the place to die in, it might have been King's College.

Two days later the Prime Minister, Stanley Baldwin, was installed as Chancellor of Cambridge University at a ceremony in the Senate House. In his speech Baldwin said, 'At the same moment that we are celebrating an occasion of historic interest to our University, and of personal happiness to some of us, that great College close by is mourning one of the greatest tragedies that have happened in the history of our University... Across the centuries like the sound of a passing bell rings the message of the Roman Emperor to his people: *principes mortales, rem publicam aeternam esse: proin repeterent sollemnia*. Princes die, but the State is eternal: let us take up our duties... The princes among men are not only statesmen; they are found in all walks of life, and I have always felt that those who go into the uttermost parts of the earth, those who attempt to scale the virgin mountains, are indeed *principes* among men. It is one of them that the University is mourning today, and it is fitting that on this occasion and from this place there should go out to his College, to his widow and to his children, a message of profound and heartfelt sympathy and affection. It is an instance today of how the State, the Republic, the University is eternal, though our great men in turn pass away.'

The flag flew at half-mast over the college, the summer ball was cancelled, the shock spread quickly to old Kingsmen, aghast and helpless. M.R. James, teller of ghost stories, wrote from Eton, 'The King's business is indeed hideous. The worst of it is, I can't believe the horrible little destroyer was mad, only desperate like a trapped rat.' In Bloomsbury the novelist E.M. Forster was lost for words, but felt the need of writing to someone 'though there is nothing one can say to anyone', and at least he would go to the funeral. Six and a half years after being married in King's chapel Sandy's ashes were placed in the crypt.

There was an inquest at which evidence was sworn, messages of condolence were passed. Swaying slightly at the events that had brought him here, stunned by the crime that had smitten him, Potts' father stepped into the witness box. He too was grimly bereft. He didn't know where he had gone wrong, he had done his best for his son – he was still doing it today – but had been dragged through fire. There was nothing he could tell the court about the company his son kept or the loneliness at the end of that short life – six blank weeks of silence till the police came and asked him to identify the body. He wouldn't show shame; he loved his son defiantly, and could only express bewilderment, desolation, and the extra hurt to his family at the hands of the press. He stepped down from the box, tired by the agony, feeling very old. He would go home and soon retire.

In our house Sandy's empty study was kept as he had left it, the fire laid with fir cones, logs, coal, ready for lighting. Every autumn Mary moved into it for a few weeks and sat among his things: stone axes and clubs, the carved prow of a dugout, an elephant's tail and antelope's horns, photos of mountains and forests, a jar of spills and feathers on the mantelpiece for lighting and cleaning his pipe, the great bookcase presiding at one end. Mary too smoked a pipe and struck matches on the fireplace tiles the way Sandy had.

Oscar Wilde wrote, 'Where there is sorrow there is holy ground,' and a sort of sanctity fell on Mary's life, though nothing could soothe the utter pain. Despite his many friends, Sandy probably wasn't easy to know and still harder to love, which made the loss so devastating. Mary once said she couldn't have survived without us children, though we were no substitute – the love for a man couldn't be turned to a child. She loved us, cared for us, brought us up serenely, bravely – a widowed mother doubling for both parents. For us she published a selection of Sandy's letters and diaries 'to preserve your father's memory', ending with a note simply that he died in his rooms at King's: 'Of this tragedy, with its waste and misery, I can neither write nor speak.'

She was a genius for holidays and in those pre-war nineteen-thirties took us to places that became beacons of the happy childhood she gave us. No doubt she wished desperately for Sandy to be travelling with us. No doubt she yearned for his comments, his vision, his love. When she talked of him a longing came into her brown eyes, a catch into her voice, as if suddenly remembering what he would have said at that moment. The ache would never go but always, it seemed, she kept something of her feelings in reserve. Something too precious ever to impart.

Then the Second World War came, bringing an extra darkness to widowhood. Mary made room in the house for evacuees – four children and, after they went to America, an elderly couple in flight from the blitz. She volunteered as an ambulance driver, practising on country roads at night with masked headlights; and worked as a postman at Christmas; and was fined a pound for breaking the blackout, a chink of light through the curtains. Sometimes she would sit at the piano and play Chopin or a nursery rhyme or folk song – *There was a lady loved a swine, The raggle-taggle gypsies, Cruel Barbara Allen.*

Then the cancer came: 'I've got this silly ulcer,' she said. Having her children round her must have multiplied the pain, the loneliness. She sent us off on holidays while she went into hospital and got us matinée tickets for London theatres – Gielgud as Shylock and Macbeth, *Watch on the Rhine*, *Arsenic and Old Lace* – with money for ices in the interval. After several operations, growing weaker, she knew at last that she would never see us grow up. We belonged to next summer, to the peace after the war, to the future she wouldn't be in; and she arranged for a sister and brother-in-law to be our guardians: 'This tiresome business,' she called it, signing her will in hospital, and came home in early spring. For a time, from a chair in the window, she watched the days grow longer while her life dwindled. The sun shone through the glass, the daffodils came up. But one day she stayed in bed – hers and Sandy's where her children were born – and died in the Easter holidays, thirteen years after Sandy. She was fifty-four; she never caught him up. On a drizzle-blown April day she led us to the cemetery and was lowered into the ground. Down there on the coffin a shiny new plate was engraved with her name and dates – a life scratched on a piece of brass. The wind snatched the priest's surplice and prayer book, a few aunts and uncles sniffed and dabbed, we children wept incomprehensively. Three teenagers wondering what came next.

For me, Sandy hadn't died as finally as this. I had known Mary as an actual person in my life and her death was an end, as real as she herself had been. But while her image slowly faded, Sandy's grew more vivid. His death was the beginning of my invention of him, a father who could never leave me. For years he hovered on the edge of things, standing in dark corners, watching at the end of my bed, sitting in an empty chair. Alone in a room, aware of him quite close, I would challenge him to make himself visible, half wanting him to, half afraid of it. What would I do if he did appear? What was he truly like?

Only the facts survived which could never make up the truth. Though I tried to find someone behind his name – searching for him, inventing him, meeting him briefly but losing him, then searching again – the authentic man escaped. I looked through his books and saw the explorer, the naturalist, the handsome face with unswerving eyes, but never caught a glimpse of fallibility to make him human, or heard his voice or felt the pressure of his hand in mine. When memory failed there was nothing but imagination. He couldn't live, or die, unless I put it into words on paper. But simple biography seemed inadequate, even immoral. Who was I to cash in on his eminent career? And that unspeakable end was nobody else's concern – did I want it bandied about as a bit of melodrama for public use? Could I exploit his tragedy for the sake of a few royalties? It seems I could. And in the process he became a character of fiction, like someone in a novel I had once written but forgotten, though I only needed to open it for the reality – the vitality and thrill of his creation – to return.

If Sandy could read this I think he would smile, but whether with approval or not I can't tell: 'By Jove, my boy, you've pinned me down.' Then the smile, with the words, would vanish.

A.F.R. Wollaston, 1924

ACKNOWLEDGEMENTS

The author would like to thank the following for their help:
Patience Bagenal, Sylvia Branford, Joanna Matthews, Miriam
Rothschild, Georgina and Francis Thompson and Sue Thompson.
Also librarians and archivists at Clifton College, King's College,
Cambridge, the Royal Geographical Society, the Natural History
Museum, the Royal Horticultural Society, the British
Ornithologists' Union, the Alpine Club and the Savile Club. But,
above all, Valerie Grove for suggesting the book in the first place
and, for their encouragement and energy, Aurea Carpenter and
Rebecca Nicolson and their colleagues at Short Books.